W9-CPN-313

So, You Want to Work with Animals?

So, You Want to Work with Animals?

Discover Fantastic Ways to Work with Animals, from **VETERINARY SCIENCE** to **AQUATIC BIOLOGY**

J. M. Bedell

BE WHAT YOU WANT *Series*

ALADDIN
New York London Toronto Sydney New Delhi

BEYOND WORDS
Hillsboro, Oregon

ALADDIN
An imprint of Simon & Schuster
Children's Publishing Division
1230 Avenue of the Americas
New York, NY 10020

BEYOND WORDS
20827 N.W. Cornell Road, Suite 500
Hillsboro, Oregon 97124-9808
503-531-8700 / 503-531-8773 fax
www.beyondword.com

This hardcover Beyond Words/Aladdin edition April 2017

Managing Editor: Lindsay S. Easterbrooks-Brown
Editor: Emmalisa Sparrow Wood
Copyeditor: Ashley Van Winkle
Proofreader: Leah Brown
Interior and cover design: Sara E. Blum
Composition: William H. Brunson Typography Services
The text of this book was set in Bembo Std.

For information about special discounts for bulk purchases, please contact Simon &
Schuster Special Sales at 1-866-506-1949 or business@simonandschuster.com.

The Simon & Schuster Speakers Bureau can bring authors to your live event. For more
information or to book an event contact the Simon & Schuster Speakers Bureau at
1-866-248-3049 or visit our website at www.simonspeakers.com.

Manufactured in the United States of America 0317 FFG

10 9 8 7 6 5 4 3 2 1

Library of Congress Cataloging-in-Publication Data
Names: Bedell, J. M. (Jane M.), author.
Title: So, you want to work with animals? : discover fantastic ways to work
  with animals, from veterinary science to aquatic biology / J. M. Bedell.
Other titles: Be what you want series.
Description: New York : Aladdin ; Hillsboro, Oregon : Beyond Words, [2017] |
  Series: Be what you want series | Audience: Ages 8-12. | Audience: Grades
  4 to 6. | Includes bibliographical references and index.
Identifiers: LCCN 2016041063 (print) | LCCN 2016044015 (eBook) |
ISBN 9781582705972 (pbk. : alk. paper) | ISBN 9781582705965 (hardcover : alk.
  paper) | ISBN 9781481472852 (eBook)
Subjects: LCSH: Animal specialists—Vocational guidance—Juvenile literature. |
  Veterinary medicine—Vocational guidance—Juvenile literature. |
  Zoologists—Vocational guidance—Juvenile literature. | Animal welfare—
  Vocational guidance—Juvenile literature. | CYAC: Vocational guidance.
Classification: LCC SF80 .B43 2017 (print) | LCC SF80 (eBook) | DDC
  636.0023—dc23
LC record available at https://lccn.loc.gov/2016041063

Let us remember that animals are not mere resources for human consumption. They are splendid beings in their own right, who have evolved alongside us as co-inheritors of all the beauty and abundance of life on this planet.

—MARC BEKOFF, PROFESSOR EMERITUS OF ECOLOGY AND EVOLUTIONARY BIOLOGY, UNIVERSITY OF COLORADO, BOULDER

CONTENTS

1

Choosing a Career Working with Animals

Congratulations on picking up a book about working with animals. Animals are a huge part of every person's life. From the foods we eat to the clothes we wear, from the simple joy of owning a pet to the complexity of fighting on the battlefield, animals are our companions, coworkers, assistants, and fellow travelers on this planet we all call home.

Why did you pick up this book, open it, and start reading? If your answer is, "Because I love animals," awesome! That's step one. But almost everyone loves animals, and those who don't love them probably really like them but don't want to take on the responsibility of owning or caring for them.

You LOVE animals. Great start. But . . . are you obsessed? Are you captivated by every dog or cat you see? Intrigued by herds of cows or horses? Fascinated by fish or whales? Does seeing an animal in need stir you to action? Do you get goosebumps just thinking about ways to protect animals in the wild? Does finding a cure for animal diseases drive you to take harder and harder science classes? Does the idea of extinction make your heart sink to your knees?

If you can answer YES! to any of those questions, or you feel that you are heading in the direction of a yes answer, then pursuing a career working with animals may be right for you.

World Leaders Have Pets Too

Barack Obama, former president of the United States, adopted a Portuguese water dog named Bo. A few years later, while still in the White House, he and his family adopted another dog named Sunny.

Bhumibol Adulyadej, former king of Thailand, had a dog named Thong Daeng, meaning "Copper," that was rescued from the streets of Bangkok. During the king's reign, he encouraged his people to adopt street dogs.

Theresa May, the prime minister of the United Kingdom, has a cat named Larry. Larry holds the official title of Chief Mouser to the Cabinet Office. When a prime minister leaves office, he or she also leaves the house at 10 Downing Street in London. The cat, however, stays.

Elizabeth II, the queen of England, loves Welsh Corgis and has owned over thirty of them during her reign.

Akihito, emperor of Japan, has a goby fish. He is an ichthyologist and has published dozens of peer-reviewed papers on fish biology. In 2006, fellow researcher Doug Hoese from Australia named his newly discovered fish Akihito in honor of his friend.

Vladimir Putin, the president of Russia, has a black Labrador named Koni. The dog was a gift from the General of the Russian Army.

SPOTLIGHT

Claude Bourgelat (1712–1779), Founder of the World's First Veterinary Schools

Claude Bourgelat was born on March 12, 1712, in Lyon, France, during the reign of Louis XIV. His father was a nobleman, and as his son, Bourgelat received an excellent education and was expected to pursue a career in law. After some time as a lawyer, he lost his focus and turned his attention to horses. Before long Bourgelat was considered the best in the nation at training and riding them. He was named the grand equerry of France and became director of the Lyon Academy of Horsemanship when he was only twenty-eight years old. The Lyon Academy was a school where young men studied horseback riding, music, math, manners, and swordsmanship.

Bourgelat soon realized that his knowledge of horse anatomy and health issues was sorely lacking, so he set out to learn as much as he could from two Lyon surgeons. Ten years later, in 1750, his book, *Élémens d'hippiatrique ou nouveaux principes sur la connoissance et sur la médecine des chevaux* (Elements of the Principles of Veterinary Art, or, New Knowledge about Medicine and Horses), was published.

The book detailed all his research into horses—research based on his own observations and experiments. The book earned him a place in the Academy of Sciences, a society that was leading the way in scientific study in Europe. In the preface, Bourgelat wrote, "Those who intend to [acquire skills in veterinary art] will not be able to acquire a sufficient degree of education . . . [since] we do not have schools for teaching."[1] It was clear that the idea of starting a veterinary school was already on his mind.

Over the next decade, it became clear to Bourgelat that educated veterinarians were needed. Thousands of cattle in herds across the country were being destroyed by a disease known as the cattle plague. It was also a time when the health of the nation's horses was critical to maintaining a powerful army and the nation's security. He convinced the government of King Louis XV that the nation needed a school of veterinary medicine, and he received the money to start one.

In 1761, the world's first veterinary college, the Royal Veterinary School of Lyon, was established. By the end of 1762, the first thirty-eight veterinary students were enrolled and beginning their studies. In 1765, Bourgelat founded the Alfort Veterinary School outside of Paris. Both colleges accepted students from throughout Europe. After graduation, those students returned to their home countries, spreading an understanding of how to use the scientific method (experience, observation, reasoning, analysis, and deduction) to study and treat diseases in animals.

As a veterinary surgeon, Bourgelat was one of the first scientists to acknowledge that the scientific study of animal biology and pathology could lead to a better understanding of human biology and pathology. This revolutionary thought is considered the point when modern medicine was born. Bourgelat is also credited with being the creator of the modern veterinary profession. He died in Paris on January 3, 1779. He was sixty-six years old.

Five Traits You Need to Work with Animals

Attentiveness

Animals can't talk. That may seem like an obvious statement, but it's important for you to understand. They don't know what you are saying to them unless you teach them. By learning to pay close attention, you will notice when an animal is happy, scared, or feeling stressed and likely to lash out. Careful attention to each animal's unique behaviors is critical to knowing how it will react in a given situation. Being attentive also helps you learn to speak cat, dog, or even dolphin, and to be in tune with what they are trying to communicate to you.

Courage

Working with animals can be very dangerous. When caring for lions in the wild, elephants in captivity, or cows on a farm, you must remember that they bite, butt, kick, and scratch. It's up to you to be prepared for any event and face their actions with calm, controlled courage. It also takes courage to euthanize an animal. Whether it's a wild animal threatening people, a sick animal in a zoo, or a wounded cat in a pet clinic, you will make life-and-death decisions many times during your career. That takes courage too.

Empathy

It's hard for an animal to understand what a human is trying to do for it. Getting a shot hurts. Having your nails clipped is scary. Being captured and put in a cage is very traumatic! Animals don't understand that a shot protects against diseases, clipped nails protect against joint damage, or being captured may protect their

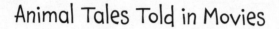

Animal Tales Told in Movies

When an intense bond is created between humans and animals it is always based on love, respect, and, most of all, trust. Here is a list of movies that depict that unique connection and the lengths people will go to to help protect the animals they love.

The Amazing Panda Adventure (1995)

Born Free (1966)

Dolphin Tale (2011)

Eight Below (2006)

Free Willy (1993)

The Horse Whisperer (1998)

Hotel for Dogs (2009)

The Journey Home (2014)

Max (2015)

Never Cry Wolf (1983)

Secretariat (2010)

Two Brothers (2004)

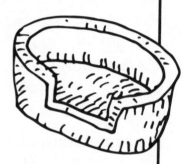

species from going extinct. Having the ability to empathize with animals will help you make appropriate decisions for them, and your job will be easier in the long run.

Patience

Animals don't understand time. In their world, it takes as long as it takes. If you want to train a horse to compete in a rodeo, a dog to sniff out drugs, or a cat to . . . wait, no one teaches cats to do anything . . . or a dolphin to perform at the aquarium, you must have patience. They learn at their own pace, and forcing them only leads to frustration for both animal and human.

The American Bison

On May 9, 2016, President Barack Obama signed the National Bison Legacy Act, which declared the American bison the United States' national mammal. The bison, saved from near extinction in the early twentieth century, joins the American bald eagle as the nation's second national animal. Besides being a national symbol, the bison is the official mammal for three states. Its image also appears on two state flags and on the seal of the Department of the Interior.

Realism

When working with animals, you must learn and adapt to what an animal can and cannot do. Be realistic about the time it takes to train them. Be realistic about the need for culling a herd or slaughtering animals for food. Be realistic about life-and-death decisions. But most of all, be realistic about their needs. Wolves and bison need huge spaces to roam. Cows and horses need pastures for grazing. Dogs are social animals and need lots of attention. As you enter a career working with animals, try to be realistic when meeting the needs of each animal in your care.

Quiz: Am I Cut Out to Work with Animals?

Let's take a quick quiz and see if you should read on and discover all the fascinating careers available working with animals.

1. When an animal pees or poops on the floor, I . . .
    a. Get a bucket and mop and clean it up.
    b. Find someone and tell them that the animal made a mess.
    c. Squeal and run away.

2. An unknown dog is running loose in my neighborhood. I . . .
    a. Ask an adult to help me catch it so we can find its owner or take it to a safe shelter.
    b. Try to catch the dog. But when it runs away, I let it go.
    c. Yell at the dog to get out of my yard!

3. I see a goat lying in the barn, separating itself from the herd. I . . .
    a. Immediately know that there is something wrong and call the vet.
    b. Watch it for a few days to see if it changes its behavior.
    c. Ignore it.

4. I had a dream about the spotted Amur leopard. In my dream I . . .
    a. Saw a future where there are thousands of leopards roaming the forests of Russia.
    b. Watched the last leopard die, and my heart broke into little pieces.
    c. Saw a leopard lying on a boulder and called out, "Get out of the way! We need those trees to build houses."

5. I see an elephant that is very sick and miserable. I'm told it won't get better. I . . .

   a. Help make it comfortable and then call a vet to euthanize it.

   b. I watch and wait, hoping it will die quickly.

   c. I walk away.

6. In school, my favorite classes are . . .

   a. Science, math, and English.

   b. Computers, economics, and marketing.

   c. Theater, physical education, and art.

7. My favorite place to be is . . .

   a. Outside; it doesn't matter what the weather is like.

   b. Inside, but I don't mind going out when the weather is nice.

   c. Inside, where I can be cozy and warm.

If most of your answers are "a," then read on. You are ready to discover all the possible careers working with animals that are open to you.

If most of your answers are "b," then read on. With a bit more education and an open mind, you can discover a career working with animals that fits you perfectly.

If most of your answers are "c," then maybe there is a different career that's right for you. But, don't give up if your heart is with animals. There are some careers in this book that might pique your interest, like animal photography. Or, you may blaze your own trail and define a special career all your own.

Things to Know If You Plan to Work with Animals

A career with animals means that you will spend much of your time working with other living creatures that require constant care. Much like human children, animals need to be carefully watched, regularly fed, given a clean place to sleep, and entertained to avoid boredom. This can be a 24-hours-a-day, seven-days-a-week job—infinitely rewarding, but sometimes grueling:

- You will work long hours, including many weekends and holidays.

- You will deal with demanding and emotional pet owners.

- You will handle frightened animals that may bite, kick, or scratch.

- You will work outside in all types of weather.

- You will deal with messy and unpleasant situations.

- You must understand that sometimes you have to euthanize an animal.

- You will face tons of paperwork.

- You must recognize and avoid compassion fatigue.

- You must understand that all animals can be dangerous, especially males and mothers with newborn babies.

US Animal Welfare Timeline

1866. The American Society for the Prevention of Cruelty to Animals is founded by Henry Bergh, a New York philanthropist and United States diplomat to Russia. The ASPCA was the first animal rights group formed in the United States and is one of the largest in the world.

1877. The American Humane Association is founded to stop the inhumane treatment of farm animals and improve their living conditions. A year later, they added the safety and protection of children to their mission.

1954. The Humane Society of America is founded to prevent cruelty to animals in laboratories, slaughterhouses, and puppy mills. Today, it is one of the largest animal activist groups in the United States, with associated animal humane societies in every state.

1955. The Society for Animal Protective Legislation is founded and becomes the first organization to lobby for humane slaughter legislation in the United States.

1966. The Animal Welfare Act is passed. The law dictates the minimum acceptable living conditions for animals in the United States, defines what mistreatment of an animal means, and sets penalties for abuse of animals.

1974. Animal Rights International is founded by Henry Spira to stop the use of animals for research and testing.

1979. The Animal Legal Defense Fund is formed to provide free legal services to animal cruelty cases. The organization is dedicated to helping create new laws, enforcing existing laws, and shaping the growing legal field of animal law.

1980. People for the Ethical Treatment of Animals is founded by Ingrid Newkirk and Alex Pacheco. The organization works for animal rights through public protests, public education, animal rescue, and lobbying for animal protection laws.

TOP DOG *profile*

Name: Rear Admiral Terri R. Clark, DVM, DACLAM
Job: Director of the Office of Animal Care and Use, Office of Intramural Research at the National Institutes of Health, and Commissioned Corps Officer with the US Public Health Service

When did you first become interested in working with animals and decide to make it the focus of your career?

I have had a love for animals for as long as I can remember. My father had a similar love and interest, and he was always bringing home dogs, cats, and even a rabbit. I also had a pet hamster at one point, and goldfish. Ultimately, my dad seemed to be the one who recognized veterinary medicine as a career choice for me, even before I was willing to acknowledge it as a possibility.

When I went to Auburn University, Alabama, for my under-graduate college program, I truly enjoyed the biological sciences and ultimately decided to pursue acceptance to Auburn's College of Veterinary Medicine.

What education/work path did you take to get to your current position with the United States Public Health Service?

I have an undergraduate degree in animal and dairy sciences and a doctorate of veterinary medicine, both from Auburn University. After graduating with my DVM, I went into private practice for a short period of time and then joined the US Army, Veterinary Corps. During my undergraduate years in college, I worked as a research technician at Auburn's veterinary college and so knew I had an interest in animal model–based research. Through the army, I was able to complete a four-year residency program in laboratory animal medicine and then took board certification exams to become a board-certified diplomate of the American College of Laboratory Animal Medicine (ACLAM).

During my twelve years with the army, I was assigned to five different research programs. Since transferring to NIH [the National Institutes of Health], I have worked primarily with the Office of Animal Care and Use (OACU). The director position required that I have a diverse animal research background and hold board certification with ACLAM. I worked as an associate director and deputy director before being hired as the director, so my years of experience supporting the NIH community were also key to my success.

Why did you decide to join the army instead of going into private practice after veterinary school?
I did work in private practice for a short time, immediately after graduating from veterinary college; however, I quickly felt that I wanted to seek a work environment that had broader professional opportunities. I entered my veterinary college program with an interest in research, and knowing that the army would also offer me the opportunity to complete additional education and training made my choice to join even easier.

You were deployed to help with the aftermath of Hurricane Katrina. What did you do during that time?
The PHS CC [Public Health Service Commissioned Corps] veterinarians assisted [relief] efforts by providing direct veterinary care and other support services to two animal shelter operations: at Lamar-Dixon Expo Center and at the Parker Coliseum at Louisiana State University, as well as directly to the State of Louisiana and the USDA.

I primarily served as the executive officer to the second veterinary team leader. As such, I served as the team leader's staff member, providing liaison and coordination to the rest of the team and visiting outlying animal shelter operations to ensure their proper constitution and support.

After Hurricane Katrina, it became clear that any disaster rescue plan needed to include a plan to rescue pets. Can you explain how your office is working to improve in this area?

Providing for pets during disasters was a very positive outcome of the devastation that occurred with the hurricanes in Louisiana; however, my office does not have authority to work with pets in a rescue situation. We do ensure all research animals held for the NIH intramural research programs are properly cared for during disasters and emergencies. Federal animal welfare laws require that we have well-developed disaster/emergency response plans, and we test those plans with tabletop exercises and the occasional actual event, such as snowstorms and power outages.

What do you see as your main responsibilities with respect to your work with/for animals?

I've recently completed my term as the chief veterinary officer (CVO) for the USPHS Commissioned Corps. As the CVO, I was responsible for providing leadership and coordination of USPHS veterinary professional affairs for the Office of the US Surgeon General and the Department of Health and Human Services. I also provided guidance and advice to the Surgeon General and the Veterinary Professional Advisory Committee on matters such as recruitment, retention, career development, and readiness of PHS veterinarians.

As people's attitudes change regarding animals used for research, can you explain how you feel about this issue and how your office is addressing their concerns?

The humane use of animals in a research setting has been influenced throughout its history by public opinion, and this influence will continue into the future. As a federal agency, our funding is provided by Congress, so our mission is set by the public influence for funding and legislature. Ultimately, it is the responsibility of my office to ensure that our programs meet the federally mandated animal welfare standards as well as our accreditation standards.

Our federal laws also require that a veterinarian with experience and training in the field of animal research be involved with the research animals' care and oversight. This is the reason my board certification exists, and it provides me with a special understanding of the needs of the research animals in this setting. Ultimately, I'm confident we are providing exceptional care and an exceptional environment for our research animals, and our collective team of scientists, veterinarians, care staff, etc. work to ensure the research we conduct is in keeping with these high ethical standards.

What future trends do you see in animal research, both using animals for research and research for the welfare of animals?
The mapping of both humans' and various animal species' genomes has led to an explosion of opportunities for biomedical research. New technologies are allowing for the genetic modeling of species beyond mice. This will give us avenues to explore that are not well supported in rodent species.

The mission of the NIH is to seek fundamental knowledge about the nature and behavior of living systems and the application of that knowledge to enhance health, lengthen life, and reduce illness and disability in humans. While animal welfare research is not our primary mission, much of what we accomplish as we strive for excellence in our daily care of research animals leads to welfare improvements. Additionally, when animal models are used for research, the outcome of the research, while focused on human health, invariably has parallel benefits for animals as well.

What tips would you give kids who are interested in pursuing a career in animal research?
It is a wonderful career that allows you to work with and care for animals and allows you to help people too. Many opportunities are available, from veterinarian and research scientist to technician and animal caretaker. All require a love of animals and science. I would encourage you to study hard in school and follow this path if science, animals, and research pique your interest and match your skills.

What is your favorite animal and why?

My favorite research animal is the mouse, with zebrafish running a close second. Scientists are able to do quite powerful genetic modelling in these two species, which has led to a tremendous level of knowledge about how our bodies and various organs and systems work and, in turn, is allowing us to understand how to address diseases and health issues.

For pets, I love my standard poodle, but have also had lovely cats, guinea pigs, fish, hamsters, and birds over the years.

|||||||||||||||||||||||||||||||||||||||||||||||||||||||||||||||||||||||||||||||||||||||||||||||||||||||||||||||||||

2

Becoming a Veterinarian

Working with animals as a veterinarian requires a variety of skills. Much like a medical doctor treats human patients, you will treat animals, but with the added burden of caring for a patient that can't tell you what's wrong or where it hurts. You will evaluate an animal's symptoms and come up with a diagnosis, set broken bones, clean wounds, and treat infections and illnesses. You will also try to prevent illness through vacinations, flea and tick control, animal care education, and owner support.

The hardest part about working with an animal is when you face the end of its life. Whether it's an exotic animal in a zoo, a patient in a veterinary clinic, or a beloved pet at home, having to decide when its life should end is a difficult and emotional task. As a veterinarian, you will face this decision often in your practice, probably every week. Be an advocate for the animal by helping the owners focus on its needs rather than their own. This takes empathy and tact.

While in high school, you should focus on college preparation classes, especially math and science. This will prepare you for the rigors of higher-level math and science classes in college. Besides that, enjoy some extracurricular activities, keep your GPA high, and study hard for the SAT/ACT exams. It's also important to get some experience with animals. Volunteer at the zoo or your local

Did you know that cats and rats can drink salt water and survive? Their kidneys separate out and dispose of the salt while the water hydrates the body, helping them survive in times of drought. Cats are also unique in that the pattern on their noses is as individual as a human fingerprint—no two cats' nose prints are the same. And, in case you didn't know, most female cats are right-pawed and most male cats are left-pawed.

humane society, work part-time for a veterinarian or in a pet store, or participate in 4-H or FFA (Future Farmers of America).

Once you get into college, you don't have to major in pre-veterinary medicine, but you do need to take advanced math and science courses. Take communication and writing classes, too. They will help prepare you for veterinary medicine school.

During your senior year in college, get ready to take the Graduate Record Examination (GRE), the Medical College Admission Test (MCAT), or the Veterinary College Admission Test (VCAT). Which one you take will depend on where you apply to veterinary medical school.

While doing all that, keep in mind that most veterinary medicine schools expect to see a minimum of four hundred hours of animal-related experience. And don't forget—join a pre-vet club! There's probably one in whichever college you choose to attend. Here is a list of places or people you can contact to get work or volunteer experience:

- 🐾 animal scientists
- 🐾 aquariums
- 🐾 humane societies
- 🐾 kennels

- 🐾 livestock farms

- 🐾 racetracks

- 🐾 sanctuaries

- 🐾 veterinarians

- 🐾 zoos

TOP DOG profile

Name: Dr. Carlos Campos
Job: Veterinarian, America's Favorite Veterinarian 2013, Owner of San Francis Veterinary Hospital

When did you first become interested in working with animals and decide to make it the focus of your career?
I have always wanted to work with animals. When I was six or seven years old, I was watching the veterinarian taking care of my dog and decided that it was what I wanted to do when I grew up.

What education/work path did you take to get to your current position?
I earned a triple major in biology, chemical science, and math education from Florida State University. While in high school and college, I volunteered in small and large animal practices in order to gain enough experience to get accepted into veterinary school. Upon graduation, I started my first job as a veterinarian at a small-animal practice.

After a year, I was offered a partnership. I worked with my partners for six years and then decided I had different ideas of how a practice should be run. I sold my shares of the practice and started planning my own hospital. While I had things in the works (many licenses must be acquired and lots of paperwork must be done prior to opening a veterinary hospital), I worked in the veterinary clinic a former classmate of mine owned in a nearby town. I opened my office, San Francis Veterinary Hospital, in March of 2010. In December 2014, I moved into a building that was twice the size of the original office to accommodate much more staff.

How and why did you choose to focus your career on domestic animals?

I had wanted to focus on rural animal medicine, but being a father to a newborn persuaded me to narrow down my field to small-animal practice. Rural animal medicine requires the doctor to be on call at all hours of the day and night. Small-animal practice allows me to work during the day and then refer after-hours emergencies to the emergency veterinary hospitals in the area.

What are some of the challenges of treating animals in your area and owning your own business?

We are a small-animal practice, but we are in a rural part of the county. So, in addition to the usual cats and dogs, we often have pigs, goats, and chickens pass through our doors. I also see pocket pets, like gerbils, guinea pigs, and sugar gliders. It can be a challenge to live and work in the same community because people recognize me when I go out to run errands. Sometimes they cannot help asking me questions about their animals' or family members' pets' issues when I am having a day off.

The American Veterinary Medical Foundation named you "America's Favorite Veterinarian" in 2013. How did you win that award and what does it mean to you?

America's Favorite Veterinarian was a contest where clients nominate their veterinarian with an essay about why they like him or her the most. One of my clients submitted her essay and, amid the hundreds of essays, they liked hers best. We were both flown to the American Veterinary Medical Association's national conference in Chicago, Illinois, for the announcement of the first America's Favorite Veterinarian Contest winner.

It was an extremely special occasion for everyone involved. It was the American Veterinary Medical Foundation's fiftieth anniversary. It was the American Veterinary Medical Association's hundreth anniversary. My client read her essay before the board members of the AVMF at a special members-only breakfast that my family and I were invited to attend. I received a beautiful plaque that is on display in my office and lots of recognition from the local and national media.

Because I won the award, my wife and I were invited to the National Hero Dogs Awards ceremony. We were flown out to Los Angeles, put up at the Hilton, and walked the red carpet. We rubbed elbows with Betty White, Lori Laughlin, and Austin Stowell. To me, the award meant that I am being recognized for doing my very best to practice veterinary medicine and my clients feel they can trust me with their four-legged loved ones. Trust between the client and myself is extremely important. We are working with patients who cannot speak for themselves. The only way to know what is wrong is through observation, testing, and careful diagnosis. I do my best to ensure that proper medical care is accessible to everyone with a pet. My philosophy is that pets enrich our lives and should not be considered a luxury.

What tips can you give students who are thinking about becoming veterinarians?

For those who want to be a veterinarian, I say, "Go for it!" Study very hard, even in high school. Get lots of exposure to animals of all kinds. Volunteer in any way you can—at a local veterinary hospital, shelter, or foster group.

Veterinary school is extremely competitive, as there are currently only thirty of them in the United States. (When I was applying, there were only twenty-six.) In order to be accepted to a school, your application must demonstrate that veterinary medicine is your passion and that you will be able to handle the course load and work. Everyone must learn about and work with all of the different types of animals. Of course you can focus on one area, but the national board exam is on all of the animals, not just your field of preference.

I thought I was going to practice rural animal medicine, but ended up doing small animals and pocket pets. There are some rural animals that come to see me occasionally, so I still get to enjoy working with them. But I do not get to go out to the farms and work in the fields as I had once imagined myself doing. It is eye-opening to see all of the different specialties and to try new things.

What is your favorite animal and why?
I cannot pick a specific animal. I like them all. However, if I were to choose a specific animal experience, it would have to be when I had the opportunity to feed and bathe a pair of rhinoceros at a local ranch. They are gentle giants.

||||||||||||||||||||||||||||||||||||||||||||||||||||||||||||||||||||||||||||||||||||||||||||||||||||||||||||||||

Veterinary Medical School

In the United States, there are thirty accredited colleges of Veterinary Medicine with an average of three thousand graduates each year. Don't let those numbers worry you. If you prepare early, it's no harder to get into a veterinary school than it is to get into a medical school. Upon graduation, you will have earned a doctor of veterinary medicine (DVM) degree.

If you'd like to study abroad, there are some veterinary medical schools you can attend. However, to practice in the United States after graduation, you must take a licensure exam. To take that exam, you have to have attended a college that is accredited by the American Veterinary Medical Association's (AVMA) Council on Education. They have accredited five veterinary colleges in Canada, four in Australia, two in the Caribbean, two in Scotland, and one each in New Zealand, Mexico, Ireland, and the Netherlands. After graduating from an accredited veterinary school, you will have to pass the North American Veterinary Licensing Exam, and probably a state exam as well.

Getting a DVM degree can open doors to a variety of career opportunities and lead to vastly different lifestyles—from a private large-animal practice in a rural area to a teaching or research position at an urban university, medical center, or industrial laboratory. Of the approximately eighty thousand veterinarians in the United States, the majority are in private practice. The rest are in a variety of careers practicing in zoos, aquariums, and sanctuaries; working for the military, the government, or in private industry; and conducting research or teaching classes at universities across the nation.

Where Doctors of Veterinary Medicine Work

- ❀ in private practice, general or specialty

- ❀ for zoos, aquariums, and animal sanctuaries

- ❀ for the federal government
  - **a.** the Department of Agriculture Food Safety and Inspection Service
  - **b.** the Centers for Disease Control
  - **c.** the National Institutes of Health

d. the Public Health Service
e. the Food and Drug Administration

- in corporate veterinary medicine

- in the United States military

- for universities, teaching and research

- for pharmaceutical companies

- in animal shelters

- as public policy consultants

- in areas of global veterinary medicine

- in areas of food supply medicine

Early Veterinary Medicine Timeline

3000 BCE. Urlugaledinna, a man from Babylonia, is the first person recorded as an "expert in healing animals." Babylonians lived on land that today is in southern Iraq.

2350 BCE. *The Shalihotra Samhita* is an encyclopedia by the Indian physician Shalihotra. The manuscript, written in Sanskrit, describes horse and elephant anatomy, types of surgery, and ways to cure and prevent diseases. It also describes how to identify the age of a horse by using its bone structure.

1900 BCE. The Papyri of Kahun are written records of Egyptian veterinary medicine. The manuscripts were discovered by Flinders

Petrie in 1889 and are housed at University College London.

460–375 BCE. Hippocrates of Kos, the father of Western medicine, was an ancient Greek physician and philosopher who wrote the Hippocratic Oath, a code of ethics adhered to by doctors of human medicine even today. Hippocrates, whose name means "chief of horses," and his brother Sosander were said to be hippiatroi, or horse doctors.

World Veterinary Day is celebrated the last Saturday in April. It was created in 2000 by the World Veterinary Association to honor the work of veterinarians around the world. Raise a paw or tap a hoof and say "Thank you" to your local vet.

384–322 BCE. Aristotle is now known as the father of biology. He was an ancient Greek philosopher who studied land and marine animals and attempted to classify them based on their physical characteristics. He also categorized them by their blood: those with red blood were vertebrates and those without blood were cephalopods. His classification methods were used for hundreds of years.

Mid- to Fourth-Century CE. Apsyrtus of Bithynia, the father of veterinary medicine, was a famous animal doctor and army officer who traveled with Constantine into war. While taking care of the horses, he discovered and described new diseases, recognized that several diseases were contagious and prescribed isolation to combat them, and successfully treated animals using splints for broken bones and stitches for open wounds.

Late Fourth Century CE. Publius Flavius Vegetius Renatus, another father of veterinary medicine, wrote *Digesta Artis Mulomedicinae*, a guide to veterinary medicine in which he

25

searched for natural causes of disease using the scientific methods of observation and documentation.

Fifth–Sixth Century CE. *The Hippiatrica* was first compiled using seven ancient veterinary manuals. The information in it included practical treatments for animal disorders and disease, as well as information on how to breed, feed, and groom horses.

Early Sixteenth Century CE. *Propertees and Medcynes for a Horse and Mascal of Oxen, Horses, Sheepes, Hogges, Dogges* is the earliest veterinary book written in English. The author is unknown.

1761 CE. **Claude Bourgelat** founded the Lyon College in France. It was the first veterinary school in the world.

Types of Veterinarians

1. **Small animal.** Small-animal veterinarians are the most common. They account for about 70 percent of veterinarian practices. They care for the health needs of family pets, mostly cats and dogs. Some also care for the more common exotic pets like ferrets, guinea pigs, and rabbits. Their main clients are people who consider their animals members of the family.

2. **Large animal.** About 16 percent of veterinarians focus their education on the care of farm animals like goats, cows, pigs, horses, and sheep. These

Equipment that Veterinarians Use Every Day

- bandages
- catheters
- latex gloves
- microchip scanner
- microscope
- muzzles
- nail trimmer
- needles
- office equipment; computers and fax machines

- razors
- scale
- scissors
- stethoscope
- syringes
- thermometer
- ultrasound equipment
- X-ray machine

animals can live on small farms, large farms, or in special facilities where they are raised and then butchered for food. Most large-animal vets have clients who raise animals for products like milk, eggs, or wool, or for food like beef, pork, or chicken.

3. **Exotic animal.** These veterinarians treat animals that require specialized knowledge. They care for reptiles and birds, "pocket animals" like mice and gerbils, or amphibians and fish.

4. **Wild animal.** These veterinarians treat any wild animal. They work for zoos, wildlife

rehabilitation centers, and animal sanctuaries. A wildlife vet treats monkeys, giraffes, lions and tigers, wild birds, aquatic mammals, or fishes.

5. **Research.** These veterinarians focus their work on clinical research. They work to find treatments for animal diseases, collect data on the health of animals in the wild or in captivity, and study individual animal species to learn as much as possible about their life cycles.

> During the week of Halloween, calls to pet poison hotlines increase by 12 percent. It is their busiest time of year, treating pets who have eaten candy or decorations.

Sometimes DVMs choose to specialize. Like human doctors, vets choose an area of focus and go through additional training to become experts in that field. That extra training may include additional schooling, internships, residency, and board certifications.

Animal-specific specialties

- avian (birds)

- beef cattle (cattle raised for meat)

- canine (dogs)

- dairy animals (cows and goats that produce milk)

- equine (horses)

- exotic companion mammals (rabbits, mice, guinea pigs)

28

- 🐾 feline (cats)

- 🐾 food animals (cattle and pigs)

- 🐾 reptile and amphibian (lizards, turtles, snakes)

- 🐾 poultry (chickens, turkeys, ducks)

Mobile veterinarian practices are becoming increasingly popular. A mobile practice is cheaper to start than a brick-and-mortar office, and you can charge a house call fee. You're not limited to a specific geographical area and can travel to where there's a demand. Busy families like the convenience, and the animals are less stressed when treated in their homes. Problems include scheduling difficulties, traffic delays, equipment limitations, and possibly working longer hours.

SPOTLIGHT

Louis J. Camuti (1893–1981), The First Cat Doctor

Louis J. Camuti was born on August 30, 1893, in Parma, Italy. His family immigrated to the United States and settled in the borough of Manhattan in New York City. As a child, Camuti had a keen interest in animals. That love was solidified when, at the age of eleven, his cat saved his life.

One day while he was bedridden with typhoid fever, a fire started in his house. As smoke filled the room, his cat jumped on the bed and began to move back and forth across his face, keeping the smoke at bay. Camuti said, "As if to clear away the smoke and protect me from the fire . . . the cat stayed on my chest until my mother rushed into my room."[1] That cat's heroic action inspired Camuti to dedicate his life to the health and welfare of cats.

He graduated from Cornell University in 1916, and when World War I began he enlisted in the 1st Cavalry New York National Guard. After his service, he enrolled in New York University and received his DVM degree. After graduation in 1920, Camuti opened his first veterinary office on Broad Street in Mount Vernon, New York.

In the early 1920s, the horse was being replaced by the automobile. Because of this transition, many New York City veterinarians were forced to change the focus of their practice from horses to other animals or move to smaller communities outside the city. Some veterinarians were beginning to treat pets, especially family dogs.

Camuti started out treating cats and dogs, but within a few years he had opened a second clinic on Park Avenue and focused his practice exclusively on cats. As the years passed, Camuti spent less time in the office and more time visiting his patients in their homes. He preferred this arrangement because he thought it eased the cats' anxiety and helped him diagnose problems more accurately. Unfortunately, Camuti soon learned that one of the challenges of going to a cat's home was its acute sense of hearing. The cats seemed to know when he was coming and would scurry away and hide. He spent many hours coaxing patients out of their hiding places.

Over the years, Camuti's reputation spread and his practice grew. He wrote a monthly column called

"Feline Practice" for a veterinary journal and coauthored two books about his life as a cat vet: *Park Avenue Vet* in 1962 and *All My Patients Are under the Bed: The Memoirs of a Cat Doctor* in 1980.

In February 1981, eighty-seven-year-old Dr. Camuti died of a heart attack on the Major Deegan Expressway while traveling to treat a patient. His daughter, Nina Danielsen, said of her father, "Until his arrival as a veterinarian, cats were mousers, something of nuisance value, to be replaced when needed, rather than to be loved or cared for. Dad came along with his own natural love for the felines and he gave dignity to them."[2]

Quiz: Name That Specialty!

Besides animal-specific specialties, DVMs can choose to focus in specific areas of animal medicine, animal welfare, or research. Here's a quiz that will help you understand some of the other career paths open to you if you choose to pursue a career as a veterinarian.

Match each description in the first list with one of the specialties in the second list.

1. I give animals medication so they feel little or no pain during surgery. I also help aggressive animals get examinations.

2. I monitor animal care facilities to make sure all animals are healthy, comfortable, and safe.

3. I observe animals and try to figure out why they behave the way they do.

4. I treat animals that have bad breath, cavities, or gum disease.

5. I treat animals that have a rash, fungus, or ear infection. I specialize in issues related to the skin.

6. When there is an accident and the family veterinarian is not available, I treat animals who need critical care.

7. I treat animals with cancer, congestive heart failure, or loss of sensation or mobility due to nervous system problems.

8. Each year, 26 million animals are used for research. I make sure those animals are treated responsibly and humanely.

9. I help develop vaccines, drugs, and other treatments for the viruses, bacteria, fungi, and parasites found in animals.

10. I research animals' dietary needs. I also help pet owners understand what they should feed their pets.

11. I treat animals that have glaucoma or other vision problems, using medication and sometimes surgery.

12. I examine tissue samples in a lab and determine whether an animal has cancer or another disease. I also conduct research on the prevention and treatment of diseases.

13. After animals are diagnosed with an illness, I prescribe medication and make sure it stays within safe and legal limits.

14. I fight the spread of zoonoses, diseases than can pass from animals to humans like rabies, West Nile virus, the avian flu, and other contagious diseases in animals.

15. I can take X-rays, CT scans, ultrasound images, and magnetic resonance images (MRIs) of animals. I look inside an animal's body to help determine a diagnosis.

16. I help animals following an injury, illness, or surgery. When a racehorse sprains its ankle or a dog breaks its leg, I find ways to return the animal to normal function.

17. I can replace a dog's hip, remove a horse's cancer, or remove a foreign object from a cat's stomach. I specialize in either large animals or small animals.

18. I provide genetic screening and breeding services for animals.

19. I know how to treat cats and dogs who eat raisins, chocolate, or rat poison. I can treat California sea lions who have eaten algae tainted with domoic acid.

20. I took extra courses and focus my work on wild animals, in captivity or in their natural habitats. When wild animals are kept as pets, I am sometimes called in to take care of them.

Specialties

a. Animal behavior
b. Laboratory animal medicine
c. Radiology
d. Nutrition
e. Pathology
f. Emergency and critical care
g. Anesthesia
h. Pharmacology
i. Surgery
j. Toxicology
k. Preventive medicine
l. Internal medicine
m. Dentistry
n. Zoological medicine
o. Theriogenology
p. Ophthalmology
q. Sports medicine and rehabilitation
r. Animal welfare
s. Microbiology
t. Dermatology

||||||||||||||||||||||||||||||||||||||||||||||||||||||||||||||||||||||||||||||||||||||||||||||||||||

Name: Hannah Whittier
Age: 15
Job (when not studying!): Future
Veterinarian

When did you first discover your love for animals?

I first discovered my love for animals at a young age. But I really knew when I was in first or second grade and I was coming home from a birthday party. We were almost home and we saw a young chickadee with an injured wing. It was hobbling all over the road. My father jumped out of the car with a basket to try to help the animal. He kept looking, but I was impatient and wanted to go home. Sadly, he could not catch the bird. We went home, and from that day on, I always wished I had helped that little bird. After that, I knew I wanted a job helping animals and keeping them healthy for the rest of my life.

Describe your experiences in the Adventures in Veterinary Medicine program at Tufts University.

I attended Tuft's Adventures in Veterinary Medicine when I was entering the seventh grade. I walked in, and I am a nervous person, but I knew there was no need to worry—I was home. When I walked in, I felt as though this is what I had looked for my whole life. It was the chance to do what I really wanted.

Day after day it got better. The classes were new and exciting. We learned things such as basic animal care and how to tip sheep [set a sheep on its rump to gain access to its belly or trim its hooves], as well as played with chickens and pigs. We attended lectures on a variety of topics, including wildlife and special-needs dogs. It was so well rounded that no matter what kind of vet you wanted to be, they could show you what it was like. One of the best parts was watching a real surgery go on. I also loved learning about the animals you got to meet along the way. But the best part is I made friends I still keep to this day. I even still see some of the counselors when I go to Tufts's open house, and they still remember me.

What advice would you give other middle grade students who are interested in working with animals?
If you are a middle school student who wants to be a vet, I would tell you to go for it, but don't be afraid to try new things. You can search all over the internet for "how to be a vet" or "animal anatomy" but—coming from someone who has looked up these things thousands of times—until you experience the real thing, nothing will compare. But never give up. At times you may feel there is nothing you can do, but if you keep working for it, you will get there. Also, keep your science and math grades up—they will really help.

If you were a veterinarian today, what animal(s) would you focus on and why?
I would work with wildlife animals, especially birds. I want to do this because they are the animals that you don't see every day, such as bears, birds, and fisher cats. I think I want to work with birds because of that one bird I could not save, and all birds just fascinate me.

What is your favorite animal and why?
My favorite animals are hawks, because they are just so swift and mysterious. But they do care for their families. I feel they are such a symbol of letting go and feeling free to be you.

What animal-related books, magazines, websites, or organizations do you enjoy?
My favorite website to use is HollyandHugo.com because they have all types of online courses that let you see more into the lives

of animals. Also, I currently visit the Cornell University website for lots of information and read lots of regular animal books and anatomy books.

Where do you see yourself in ten years?

I see myself graduating from Cornell University in upstate New York. Also, I'll be ready to go out into the field of wildlife medicine, so hopefully I'll be working as a successful veterinarian for a park, Tufts, or in my own practice. I also would like to volunteer to help out organizations such as ASPCA and maybe adopt a few animals along the way.

||||||||||||||||||||||||||||||||||||||||||||||||||||||||||||||||||||||||||||||||||||||||||||||||||||||||||||

Working with Domestic Animals

If becoming a veterinarian doesn't seem right for you, there are other career paths you can take and still work with animals. In the next several chapters, you will see many career possibilities that require less schooling, which means you will have lower tuition costs and can enter the job market more quickly. You won't have the responsibilities or income of a veterinarian, but you will be able to have a career working with animals. Many of these career paths require that you have some schooling or be registered, licensed, or certified according to the requirements of the state in which you live.

Most jobs for technologists and technicians are found in local animal hospitals, clinics, and shelters. But, there are some really neat places where you could work if the stars align and you have the right education and experience:

- 🐾 Sea World in California

- 🐾 Walt Disney World's Animal Kingdom

- 🐾 Ringling Bros. and Barnum & Bailey circus

- Popular zoos like the San Diego Zoo and the Bronx Zoo

- Noah's Ark in Georgia

- Woodstock Farm Animal Sanctuary in New York

Why do some animals' eyes glow at night? Because they have an additional layer called a tapetum underneath the retina. The tapetum acts like a mirror, reflecting light back through the animal's retina to enhance its night vision.

A chameleon's eyes sit high on the head and can move independently. This allows it to see in two directions at the same time, swiveling each eye around in search of prey. Once it sees something to eat, both eyes focus sharply like high-powered binoculars, giving it great depth perception so its sticky tongue can snatch up a tasty meal.

And, did you know that starfish have eyes? They do. Five of them, one on the end of each arm. Unfortunately, their simple-structured ocelli can only sense light.

Veterinary Technologists and Technicians

Veterinary technologists have a bachelor of science degree in veterinary science or veterinary technology and usually work in advanced research under the guidance of a scientist or veterinarian. They work in laboratories at universities or research facilities. A veterinary technologist degree can be earned at twenty-three accredited colleges in the United States, with another thirteen colleges awaiting accreditation. Technologists also work in private-practice animal clinics.

Veterinary technicians are graduates of two- or three-year programs in veterinary technology and have earned an associate's degree or a certificate. Technicians must pass the Veterinary Technician National Exam (VTNE), which is a four-hour exam with two hundred multiple-choice questions that cover seven main areas of knowledge: surgery preparation and assistance, dental procedures, laboratory procedures, animal nursing, drugs, medical testing equipment, and anesthesia. Technicians usually work for a veterinarian in a clinical setting, but some work in laboratories.

Depending on the clinic or laboratory, the veterinarian or scientist, and the individual's level of training, technologist and technician responsibilities can overlap. Here are some general responsibilities for both:

- administer anesthesia and monitor the animal while it's unconscious

- bathe animals, clip nails and claws

- explain an animal's condition to owners

- explain prescribed medications to the animal's owners

- give vaccinations and medications prescribed by the veterinarian

- help with diagnostic tests, like X-rays or CT scans

- perform urinalyses tests or blood counts

- prepare tissue samples and collect blood or urine samples

- provide dental care

- provide emergency first aid

- provide nursing care following surgeries or procedures

- record an animal's vital information and medical history

- restrain animals during exams

Like veterinarians, technologists and technicians can specialize in specific animals like small animals, exotic animals, or wild animals. Or they can choose a specific area of animal care like dentistry, anesthesia, emergency or critical care, surgery, animal behavior, or zoological medicine.

 # SPOTLIGHT

Ian Dunbar, (1947–), The Father of Puppy Socialization

Ian Dunbar was born on April 15, 1947, and grew up on his family's farm in England. While Dunbar was still a young boy, his grandfather taught him that touching any animal was an earned privilege, not a right. From that first lesson in animal behavior, he built a career on teaching others the best ways to train and treat their furry friends.

After high school, Dunbar attended the Royal Veterinary College in London, where he earned his veterinary degree and was given special honors degrees in physiology and biochemistry. Later, he earned his PhD in animal behavior from the University of California,

Berkeley. He spent years researching how dogs use their sense of smell to communicate, how they understand their place in human and canine societies, and the reasons they become aggressive.

In 1982, Dunbar opened the Sirius Dog Training school, where he taught the world's first off-leash puppy socialization and training classes using techniques that are universally recognized and followed today. Many people credit him with ushering in the modern era of dog training.

In 1993, he organized the K-9 GAMES in San Francisco. The K-9 GAMES use team competition to help dogs and their owners have fun together, while teaching owners simple training techniques. Although the games are no longer held in the United States, they are still popular in France and Japan. In that same year, he founded the Association of Professional Dog Trainers, which focuses on sharing information with dog trainers and encouraging them to keep educating themselves about new and better training techniques.

Dunbar has written for the *American Kennel Club Gazette*, founded the Animal Behavior Department of the San Francisco Society for the Prevention of Cruelty to Animals, written many dog behavior books, and appeared on popular television shows in England, the United States, and Japan. He is also a member of several societies, including the Royal College of Veterinary Surgeons and the International Society for Applied Ethology (the science of animal behavior).

While traveling along his dog-loving path, he met and married Kelly Gorman, the cofounder and president of Open Paws, a nonprofit dedicated to finding happy homes for cats and dogs. Today, he continues to work tirelessly for the welfare of dogs by lecturing at conferences, writing books, consulting for movies like Pixar's *UP*, and teaching seminars and workshops around the world.

As the first to recognize and then promote the early socialization of puppies, Dunbar has earned the title "father of puppy socialization." Most dog owners now know that their puppies must be introduced to as many people and situations as possible in the first three to twelve weeks of life. If you wait until they are older, they may develop behavior problems. Because of Dunbar's dedication, millions of dogs and their owners have learned how to peacefully and happily coexist.

Veterinary Assistants and Laboratory Animal Caretakers

Veterinary assistants work for veterinarians in animal hospitals and clinics, while laboratory animal caretakers work for scientists in laboratories where animals are kept for research. Working in either position means that you are on the front line of animal care. You are responsible for meeting many of the animals' basic needs and making sure they are treated humanely. Like technologists and technicians, you can work in all the specialty areas, including large-animal, exotic-animal, and wild-animal practices.

Additional education beyond high school is not required for these positions, and much of what you need to know is taught on the job. If you would prefer to have some training, there are schools that offer one-year certificates. That certificate may help you land a job in more competitive areas, like working with wild animals. Job responsibilities differ from state to state and from clinic to clinic. Here is a list of some basic responsibilities:

- answering phones and scheduling appointments

- clerical work, including collecting payments

- exercising and grooming animals

- feeding, watering, changing bedding, and handling animals

- greeting and signing in patients

- observing animal behavior and watching for anything unusual

- ordering and taking inventory of supplies

- preparing and cleaning surgery suites

- preparing, cleaning, and maintaining equipment

||||||||||||||||||||||||||||||||||||||||||||||||||||||||||||||||||||||||||||||||||||||||||||||

Name: Abbigail Hickman
Age: 12
Job (when not studying!): Owner and Fundraiser at Pins for Pets

YOUNG PUP *profile*

When did you first discover your love for animals and decide that they needed your help?

Ever since I was little, I've loved animals. I've grown up with them. When I was nine, I went to the old Tracy animal shelter to adopt a cat. I was taken aback by the condition of the shelter. From the freeway it looked like abandoned concrete trailers. To top it all off, it was right next to a sewer treatment plant. It smelled horrible! I was really upset. I ran to my mom and told her that she had to do something. She told me, "No, you have to do something." So I did something.

What was your first project to help save dogs and cats in need?

My very first project was a bowling tournament. I have been bowling since I was six, so I knew about the many bowling tournaments that go on at West Valley Bowl. I talked to the manager, and he said I could do a bowling tournament.

When and why did you decide to start Pins for Pets, and what do you hope to achieve?

I started Pins for Pets to try and help the Tracy animal shelter with everything they needed. I gave them food, toys, treats, and other things that they needed so they wouldn't have to take it out of their funds to help sick animals.

Describe your fundraising campaigns.

My bowling tournament usually gets around $10,000 a year. I don't charge any money for my Welcome Home kits, so I pay for them through some of the money from my fundraiser. The rest goes to the animal shelter. Sometimes the Stockton Heat [a professional ice hockey team] will let me set up a booth at their games. My parents and my friend Andrew are my greatest supporters. They help me with everything I do. I'm very thankful to have them.

I've received many awards for my work and I'm grateful for all of them. One that has helped me a lot is the Nickelodeon HALO Effect award. I got to go to New York and appear on the HALO Awards. They gave me $5,000 for my company. With that $5,000, I was able to start my Welcome Home kits program.

Describe your favorite experience with an animal.

My favorite experience with an animal has to be when I played hide-and-seek with my sister's goats. They were only six months old, and they were adorable.

We love our animals! And that means we strive to find ways to celebrate them or call attention to issues that impact their lives. One way we do this is by declaring a national appreciation day. Here's a list of some of the many animal appreciation days that mark our calendar each year:

April 10—Farm Animals Day was established to campaign for the humane treatment of livestock and to find homes for abused or abandoned farm animals.

May, third Friday—Endangered Species Day is set aside to teach people about the need to protect those wild animals that are in danger of going extinct and the importance of protecting their habitats.

August 26—Dog Day is celebrated to honor man's best friend and to raise awareness of the need to care for homeless and abused dogs. The National Dog Day Foundation uses this day to discourage unethical breeding and promote adoption.

October 21—Reptile Awareness Day was created to highlight the important role reptiles play in keeping ecosystems healthy by eating bugs and rodents. Many of the world's reptiles are nearing extinction because people are stealing their eggs and destroying their habitats.

October 29—Cat Day is dedicated to raising awareness of the domestic cat. The American Society for the Prevention of Cruelty to Animals uses this day to promote the adoption of cats and to bring attention to the growing problem of feral cat colonies.

What books or organizations do you enjoy?
I enjoy lots of books, but a really good one is *Old Yeller*. It's really sad, however, so be warned. A really good organization (other than my own) is ASPCA.

Where do you see yourself in ten years?
In ten years I would just have graduated from college, so I would probably be starting to take my business nationwide, or I might possibly want to become a farmer or something working with animals.

Careers with Domestic Animals

Animal control officers/animal cruelty investigators are on the front line of animal protection. They inspect kennels, stables, farms, and pet shops to make sure that all animals are treated humanely. They investigate reports of cruelty and can make arrests. They help enforce licensing laws and catch stray domestic animals or dangerous out-of-their-native-habitat wild animals. Most are employees of local or county governments and may assist police or fire departments when there's an animal involved in an incident.

Most training happens on the job, but some coursework in animal science could help you land a job. Some states require certification. The National Animal Care and Control Association offers certification classes across the nation. They encourage animal control officers and investigators to understand the laws in their state and seek professional training in areas like animal capture techniques, animal first aid, and animal behavior.

Boarding kennel owners and workers care for animals while their owners are away on business or vacation. From the time an animal enters their care, they are responsible for feeding, watering, grooming, and exercising it. They also play with the animals and keep them from getting lonely. Kennel workers clean cages and give daily reports on each animal's health and behavior.

Breeders work with a variety of animals. They may breed purebred cats or dogs, high-yield milking cows, racehorses, or exotic animals in captivity. To breed small animals, you don't need special training. What you do need is a concern for their well-being and an understanding of animal genealogy and artificial insemination techniques. To work with exotic animals, you will need a bachelor's degree in veterinary science and possibly a graduate degree in zoology. To work with farm animals, pursue a four-year degree in animal science.

Dog walkers are hired to take dogs out for walks one or more times a day. They may work for a company or as independent contractors. As a dog walker, you must be confident that you can handle your charges in any situation. You should know basic doggie first aid and be willing to stay on your feet for long periods of time. The upside is that the dogs are always happy to see you; the downside is that you have to pick up their poop.

Pet sitters are hired when owners want to go on a trip but keep their pets in their home. Besides being a dog walker, they care for the dog's (or other animal's) needs, including feeding it, playing with it, and making sure it gets outside to relieve itself. Pet sitters may also double as house sitters. Some pet sitters may care for farm animals by collecting chicken eggs, exercising horses, or feeding goats.

Pet store employees work with animals that live in a store until they are bought. They must learn how to keep cages clean, and they feed, water, and care for many different animals, including puppies, kittens, reptiles, snakes, rodents, and even spiders, fishes, and insects. As a pet store employee, you need to have basic knowledge of each animal so you can educate people who come in to purchase them.

While it's universally agreed that dogs evolved from wolves, the exact area on the planet where they originated is still up for grabs. With cats, it's settled. Their origins can be traced to five female wildcats that lived ten thousand years ago in the Near East. Those five cats are the original mothers of all 600 million domestic cats alive today. And, in case you didn't know, the domestic cat is a menace. They are responsible for the extinction of at least thirty-three different species, including birds, mammals, and reptiles. Cats are listed as one of the top one hundred invasive species!

Quiz: Guess Who Sleeps Here

Getting a good night's sleep is important for every living creature. Some animals, like aardvarks and skunks, are nocturnal, which means they sleep during the day. Others, like squirrels and honeybees, are diurnal, which means they sleep at night. And then there are the crepuscular animals, like cats and deer. They sleep during the day and night but are active at dawn and dusk.

Marine mammals, like dolphins and whales, sleep with one-half of their brains at a time. The other half remains awake so they can continue to breathe and swim. Fire ant workers take short one-minute naps 253 times each day. And, watch out below! Albatrosses can sleep while they fly!

Just like you want to sleep in your own bed, animals seek a place that is comfortable and safe from predators. Below is a list of places where animals sleep. Can you match the place with the animal who sleeps there?

48

1. I sleep in a hollow log, but seldom the same one for more than a few nights.

2. I sleep hanging upside down in a cave.

3. I sleep in a paw-made bed in a den. In the winter, I sleep for months in a state called hibernation.

4. I sleep in the water, wrapped in kelp and holding hands with a friend.

5. I sleep in the water with my tusks hooked into the ice so I don't float away.

6. I sleep in an underground chamber, on my back, with my legs in the air. Sometimes I snore.

7. I sleep while gliding through the air.

8. I sleep in a row with others. If I am on the end of the row, I sleep with one eye open.

9. I sleep on a platform bed that I make myself in the forest canopy.

10. I sleep in ant and termite nests after I eat them all.

Critters

a. Alpine swift
b. Opossum
c. Chimpanzee
d. Wombat
e. Bear

f. Aardvark
g. Walrus
h. Duck
i. Sea otter
j. Bat

Answers: 1: b 2: j 3: e 4: i 5: g 6: d 7: a 8: h 9: c 10: f

49

TOP DOG *profile*

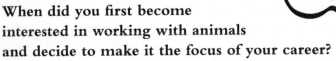

Name: Christeen Allestad
Job: Technician Assistant at Companion
Pet Clinic of Forest Grove

When did you first become interested in working with animals and decide to make it the focus of your career?

Even as a young kid, I knew I was interested in animals. Most people I've worked with have said the same thing. I started making it the focus of my career when I was in college and I was volunteering at an animal shelter.

What education/work path did you take to get to your current position?

I volunteered a lot at first. I cleaned kennels at a couple shelters. I job shadowed at a clinic. I was finally offered a job as a receptionist in a clinic. It was a small clinic, so I had opportunities to learn more. As I learned more, I started helping more animals. I'm currently taking online classes to get my certification to be a CVT [Certified Veterinary Technician].

What is the hardest part of your job?

There can be a lot of hard parts. Veterinary medicine doesn't pay well compared to a lot of other industries. You get scratched, bit, and urinated and defecated on. But the part I have the hardest time with is euthanasia. You have to put on a brave face and comfort a family about the hardest decision to make as a pet owner, holding their pet with them as they help it find a pain-free passing.

What part of the job do you enjoy the most?

I love getting to know the clients and their families. It really gives me a sense of community. When I recognize a patient walking in the door, I get excited.

How do you know that this is the right career for you?
We see some clients who come in convinced that they absolutely cannot help their pet and are prepared to say their final goodbyes. When we're able to help the patient, the look of relief and hope on the owner's face always makes this job worth it.

What tips would you give kids who are interested in pursuing a career working with animals?
Get good grades in school. The better-paying jobs require getting a certificate or, as a veterinarian, a postgraduate degree. There's a lot of learning involved, so you might as well get used to it. Volunteering can be a great way to build up experience and get your foot in the door. Many veterinary programs value life experiences gained by working with animals.

What is your favorite animal and why?
I always have a hard time with that question, I love them all so much for different reasons I can never just pick one. My cat is pretty spoiled rotten, though.

Caring for Wild Animals

If working with domestic animals is too tame for you, then maybe you'll be interested in one of the many careers working on the wild side of animal care. There are wild animals all over the world, from the smallest featherwing beetle to the largest blue whale. In this chapter, you'll learn about jobs working with wild mammals that roam the earth and swim in the ocean. If you're interested in bugs, birds, or fishes, you can read about them in chapter 6.

One of the wildest animals on earth is the snapping shrimp, or pistol shrimp. It has a gigantic claw that can shoot jets of water at 105 feet per second—more than 70 miles per hour—creating a stream of bubbles that explode at 210 decibels (a gunshot is 150). The water instantly heats to 8,000 degrees Fahrenheit (water boils at 212 degrees Fahrenheit at sea level), and there is a bright flash of light. This shockwave stuns or kills the shrimp's prey. The shrimp can also use this ability to tunnel into rock to build a safe place to hide.

In Zoos and Aquariums

The first place you probably think of when discussing where to find wild animals is a zoo. There are over ten thousand animal collections open to the public around the world, and 212 accredited zoos in the United States. About 175 million people visit zoos each year, and you were counted as one of them when you went to the zoo with your family or on a school field trip.

The second place you will find wild animals is in an aquarium. There are 240 marine aquariums or ocean life centers around the world, and 79 of those are in the United States. Many of the jobs you find in a zoo will be the same in an aquarium. In a zoo you will work with mammals, reptiles, and birds. In an aquarium you will work with sea turtles, dolphins, and jellyfish. However, to work in an aquarium, you need to love the water, know how to swim, and plan on getting your self-contained underwater breathing apparatus (scuba) certification.

World's Largest Zoos

1. Berlin Zoological Garden in Germany with 1,504 species on 84 acres

2. Henry Doorly Zoo and Aquarium in Nebraska with 962 species on 130 acres

3. Beijing Zoo in China with 950 species on 220 acres

4. Columbus Zoo in Ohio with 793 species on 580 acres

5. London Zoo in England with 755 species on 36 acres

World's Largest Aquariums

1. **The Georgia Aquarium** in the United States is the largest aquarium in the world, with over one hundred thousand sea creatures. Its largest tank is home to whale sharks and holds 6.3 million gallons (24 million liters) of water.

2. **The Dubai Aquarium and Underwater Zoo** in the United Arab Emirates has thirty-three thousand sea creatures in a gigantic tank that holds 2.64 million gallons (10 million liters) of water.

3. **The Okinawa Churaumi Aquarium** in Japan has twenty-one thousand sea creatures. Its main tank, the Kuroshio Sea, holds 1.98 million gallons (7.5 million liters) of water.

4. **L'Oceanogràfic** in Spain has forty-five thousand sea creatures in the largest tank in Europe. Two of its nine underwater towers, joined together by an underwater tunnel, hold 1.85 million gallons (7 million liters) of water.

5. **Turkuazoo** in Turkey has about ten thousand sea creatures in twenty-nine tank exhibits, the largest of which holds 1.32 million gallons (5 million liters) of water.

Zoo or Aquatic Veterinarian

To work as a zoo or aquatic veterinarian, you must first get your DVM degree, pass the North American Veterinary Licensing Exam, and pass any licensing requirements for your state. After that, you need work experience with exotic or marine animals. You get this through internships, possibly during veterinary school or immediately after. Your internship will probably last a year and set the stage for getting into a residency program.

Residency is a three- to four-year program that ends with an American College of Zoological Medicine Certification. During residency, you will gain in-depth knowledge of zoological medicine, which includes very important clinical and research skills. Some residency programs award a master's degree in specialized veterinary medicine when completed.

If you decide to become a zoo or aquatic veterinarian, you need to know that the field is competitive. Plan to work long hours, deal with challenging patients from spiders and elephants to stingrays and sharks, and face potentially dangerous situations. You are working with wild animals, including some that are willing to kick, bite, sting, and in other ways hurt you!

SPOTLIGHT

John "Jack" Hanna (1947–), Conservationist and Director Emeritus of the Columbus Zoo and Aquarium

Jack Hanna was born on January 2, 1947, in Knoxville, Tennessee. When he was five, his family moved to a farm that his father named *Bu-Ja-Su*, after the kids (Bush, Jack, and Sue). During his first years on the farm, Hanna discovered a love for animals that would dominate the rest of his life. The remote farm was his playground. He rode horses, raised bluegills in the bathtub, learned how to milk cows, collected goats, pigs, rabbits, and birds, and played with his two collies, Lance and Vandy.

One day, he rode with his father to take the dogs to the vet and met Dr. Warren Roberts, a private-practice and Knoxville Zoo veterinarian who would become one of the most influential people in Hanna's life. Hanna was fascinated by everything Dr. Roberts did.

He followed the veterinarian around whenever he came to the farm to care for their animals. Later, he hung out at the Knoxville Animal Clinic just so he could watch the doctor work.

When Hanna was eleven, Dr. Roberts finally allowed him to start cleaning cages for around forty cats and dogs. He loved the job! And Dr. Roberts was so impressed by his willingness to do the smelly, dirty work without complaining that he started giving him more opportunities and responsibilities. Hanna got to observe surgeries, accompany the doctor on trips to farms, and help deliver calves. By the time he was thirteen, he was opening the clinic each morning and caring for the animals before the doctor arrived. Dr. Roberts also took Hanna to the Knoxville Zoo, where he introduced him to the practice of wild animal veterinary medicine.

After high school, Hanna attended Muskingum College and graduated in 1968 with a bachelor of arts degree in business and political science. He opened a pet store and petting zoo, worked for a wildlife adventure company, and then, in 1973, started his zoological career as the director of the Central Florida Zoo.

In 1978, Hanna moved his family to Ohio and began work as the director of the Columbus Zoo, renamed the Columbus Zoo and Aquarium in 1999. He took that small, run-down zoo and transformed it into a nationally recognized zoological park. He increased attendance by promoting new and entertaining events, raising awareness and soliciting funds, and changing the exhibits from cages to natural habitat exhibits.

In 1986, one of the zoo's gorillas gave birth to twins. The story reached the national news programs, and Hanna was invited to appear on Good Morning America. That opened the door to more and more appearances, and soon Hanna was the go-to wildlife expert on national television. Over the years, Hanna has hosted his own television shows, written several books, and worked tirelessly to educate the public about the wondrous animals that populate the earth and the need to protect them and their habitats. Hanna, whose nickname is Jungle Jack, lives in Ohio with his wife, Suzi.

Things Zoo and Aquatic Veterinarians Do

- anesthetize animals

- check and clean teeth

- collaborate with other vets on projects like conservation or reproduction

- euthanize animals when necessary

- give vaccinations

- help plan new exhibits

- introduce animals into the wild

- oversee the care of infants if they're abandoned by their mothers

- perform preventative care checkups and new animal health screenings

- perform surgery, in the hospital or in the animal enclosure

- prescribe medications

- 🐾 publish academic papers

- 🐾 take blood samples and X-rays

- 🐾 train other veterinarians

- 🐾 treat diseases, infections, and injuries

Zookeeper or Aquarist

The focus of any zookeeper or aquarist is the care and well-being of the animals that live in the zoo, safari park, or aquarium. The work is mostly routine and includes feeding, bathing, and exercising the animals. Each animal will have a specific care plan that is crucial to follow. Another important part of the job is to monitor the animals and watch for any signs of sickness or injury and report it to the veterinarian. Since this job requires constant contact with wild animals, the same dangers exist for bites, stings, and kicks. Plan to work long hours, including nights, weekends, and holidays.

Some zookeepers and aquarists focus on an individual species like dolphins, while others focus on a group like primates, reptiles, or marine mammals. To get a job, you will need a bachelor's degree in biology, zoology, zoo technology, or other animal-related field, and some experience with wild or exotic animals.

Things Zookeepers and Aquarists Do

- 🐾 basic veterinary care

- 🐾 clean enclosures

- 🐾 communicate with the veterinarians

- educate the public about the animals

- feed and water animals

- keep notes on eating habits

- make enrichment items like puzzle feeders and frozen treats

- restrain animals for treatment

- train the animals

- watch and record odd behaviors

Other Zoo or Aquarium Jobs

Animal curators manage an institution's animal collections and exhibits. They are involved in breeding animals, buying or acquiring new animals, and designing and maintaining new and existing exhibits. In larger zoos, there may be several curators, like a curator of mammal exhibits and a curator of rainforest exhibits. In an aquarium, there could be a curator for fishes and a curator for marine mammals. A curator position requires a bachelor's degree in animal biology or a related field. Some places may require a master's degree as well.

Animal physiologists evaluate animal housing to make sure each exhibit meets ideal temperature, humidity, and space requirements for each specific animal's health and well-being. They also work in laboratories, where they study and analyze animal tissue.

Commissary keepers prepare, assemble, and distribute food to the animals. They deliver the food on a strict schedule. Some may

No wild animal should be kept as a pet. Ignore any story you hear about someone who did it and it turned out great. Most of the time, it's dangerous for you and for the animal. Wild animals require special care, can carry a variety of diseases, and are often captured in cruel and inhumane ways. If you get one, you are helping support the exotic pet trade, an industry that causes suffering to millions of animals and is leading to the extinction of some endangered species. And the best reason of all to not own one—it's illegal in most places! Here is a list of just some of the animals that should remain in the wild:

- Alligators and crocodiles grow from tiny and cute to big and ugly! One bite could take off a limb, or a swift hit from a tail can kill you.

- Bears look cute, but they are not cuddly. They can hurt or kill you with a single swipe of a paw.

- Big cats like lions and tigers look soft and cuddly, but they are unpredictable and will attack by going for the throat.

- Venomous snakes are pretty, but they can poison or kill you with a single bite. Cobras can blind you by spitting in your eyes.

- Primates like monkeys and chimpanzees look a lot like us, but they can go into a wild rampage without warning. They have no conscience, and it won't bother them if they kill you.

- Wolves and coyotes may look like dogs, but they cannot be trusted. Their instinct is to hunt, and when they feel threatened, they won't hesitate to attack.

help feed the animals according to animal behavior enrichment protocol by scattering it, freezing it in a chunk of ice, or putting it inside an object or toy.

 **Nutritionists** oversee the diets of animals in captivity. They design feeding programs for hundreds of species and make sure they eat enough of all the right things. They help animals gain or lose weight. They change diets for animals that are sick, pregnant, or lactating. They are also responsible for food safety.

The Early History of Zoos

3500 BCE. Hierakonpolis, Egypt, one of the largest urban centers of the time, housed the world's first animal collection. Archeologists discovered the site in 2009, and it contained the remains of 112 creatures, including hippos, antelopes, elephants, and baboons.

2500 BCE. Egyptian and Mesopotamian wall carvings show that rulers and wealthy people collected animals like elephants, dolphins, and giraffes and hired handlers to care for them.

1500 BCE. Queen Hatshepsut of Egypt established the first official zoo.

1000 BCE. Wen Wang, the emperor of China, created the Garden of Intelligence. It was an exhibit on 1,500 acres of land where animals were on public display in cages. The main exhibit was the giant panda.

1100 CE. King Henry I of England kept a collection of exotic animals in the Royal Park of Woodstock. When he died, they were moved to the Tower of London. The Tower Menagerie was opened to the public in the sixteenth century and closed in 1835.

1520 CE. Spanish explorer Hernando Cortes discovered Montezuma's zoo in the Aztec capital of Tenochtitlan, site of modern-day Mexico City. It was huge and required three hundred keepers to care for all the animals.

1752 CE. The Tiergarten Schonbrunn in Vienna, Austria, opened. It is the oldest zoo still operating today.

1828 CE. The London Zoo opened. It is considered the first modern zoo, designed not just to entertain the upper classes, but to allow normal citizens to see the animals and scientists to study them.

1853 CE. The first public aquarium, the Fish House, opened as part of the London Zoo.

1890 CE. The first American zoo opened in Philadelphia, Pennsylvania, with three thousand guests on the first day. The Civil War had delayed the zoo's opening for fifteen years.

1924 CE. The Association of Zoos and Aquariums was founded. It set the first standards for the care and welfare of animals in captivity.

‖‖

TOP DOG *profile*

Name: Riley Wilson, DVM
Job: Wildlife Veterinarian, Commercial Fisherman, Owner of the Pet Stop
Learn about Riley Wilson's work as a commercial fisherman in chapter 6.

When did you first become interested in working with animals and decide to make them the focus of your career?

I always wanted to be a human surgeon like my father. During my senior year in college, I helped him with a project where humans can get a particular life-threatening parasitic infection. One of my dad's coworkers on the project was a veterinarian. Through their inspiration, I decided to pursue my dream to become a wildlife veterinarian.

What education/work path did you take to get to your current position?

I received my BS in biology from Whitworth College in Spokane, Washington. Then my master's degree in environmental science and DVM from Washington State University in Pullman, Washington.

Describe your work at the Alaska Zoo.

I have been the veterinarian for the Alaska Zoo for thirty years. This involves routine exams, vaccinations and blood work, evaluations of any new arrivals to the zoo, and medical and surgical treatment for any problem that develops.

As a zoo vet, what is the hardest part of your job and what do you find the most rewarding?

I have been extremely blessed to have had the opportunity to take care of the zoo animals for my entire career. Some of my most memorable experiences have been taking care of a baby seal in our bathtub, performing a cryptorchid castration on an adult Siberian tiger, and caring for abandoned wolf pups. In addition, I was the head veterinarian in Valdez during the *Exxon Valdez* oil spill in 1989. This was extremely sad to see these oiled animals, but very gratifying to help with the project. [The *Exxon Valdez* was an oil tanker that ran aground in Alaska's Prince William Sound, rupturing its hull and spilling nearly 11 million gallons of oil into Prudhoe Bay. Twenty-eight types of animals, plants, and habitats were injured. Exxon says it spent $2.1 billion on the cleanup. According to the National Oceanic and Atmospheric

Administration, over twenty-five years later, most of the animals and habitats have recovered or are recovering. However, killer whales, herring, and several bird species have not recovered.][1]

Describe your polar bear research.
The polar bear work is conducted by the US Fish and Wildlife Service. The purpose of this work is to evaluate the health status and population of the polar bear in the Chukchi Sea. We fly out in helicopters. Polar bears are darted [a way to tranquilize them, putting them to sleep, so they can be safely handled] and their health exams are done, which includes getting their weights, taking blood samples, tagging them, and putting a tracking collar on the adult females.

What tips do you have for kids who are interested in pursuing a career as a wild animal vet?
After veterinary school, I think it is very helpful to work in a busy small-animal practice to develop your surgical skills. While you're in practice, volunteer to assist with any wildlife agency.

What is your favorite animal and why?
I enjoy all of the animals at the zoo, but especially the wolves, because they love to interact with the people they know.

In Safari or Wildlife Parks

Safari parks, also known as wildlife parks, are similar to zoos except the people are confined and the animals roam free. The animals wander in huge enclosed areas that mimic their natural habitat, and safari visitors observe them from protected walkways or vehicles. Wildlife parks still have some of the tourist attractions that you would find in zoos, like restaurants, gift shops, and park-related exhibits.

There are many jobs in safari parks, but few of them allow you to work directly with the animals. The positions that do allow you to work with animals have many of the same job titles as the zoo and acquarium careers listed above.

Wildlife Veterinarians

Wildlife veterinarians follow the same education path as zoo veterinarians. The difference is that after graduation, they must specialize in the care of animals living in the wild. They must know the anatomy of hundreds of wildly different animals and the difference between normal and abnormal behaviors. Wild animals have a built-in survival instinct that makes them hide any illness or injury for as long as possible. Because of this instinct, it is critical that wildlife vets learn to recognize subtle changes in behavior. It also means that when an illness or injury is detected, it is in a more advanced, critical stage and often requires emergency care.

||||||||||||||||||||||||||||||||||||||||||||||||||||||||||||||||||||||||||||||||||||||||||||||||||||

Name: Alexa Montegna
Age: 17
Job (when not studying!):
Founder of the Green Environment
Conservation Organization

When did you first discover your love for animals and decide that you wanted to work with them?
I grew up in a household that always had one critter or another running around. My family is very outdoorsy, which probably helped fuel my passion for animals and nature. I have always loved

animals, but like most kids, I went through all the "career phases." First and foremost, I claimed that I wanted to be a veterinarian; then I jumped around to lawyer, astronaut, businesswoman, and finally landed back on what I knew was the right choice, veterinarian.

I believe I was about eleven when I started implementing actions to help make a difference and prepare myself for this career. This was the first time that I went to Walk with the Animals, a fundraiser to raise money for our local animal shelter. After making my rounds throughout our community, I had managed to raise $600, and would continue this tradition every year after that. The event itself hosts hundreds of dogs and other animals from all over town, which really opened my eyes up to the world of animal care. Since then, I have participated in programs that allowed me to further my interest in veterinary medicine and nurture my love of animals.

Describe your experiences in the San Diego Zoo Corps.
Zoo Corps is a volunteer program for select teens, ages thirteen to seventeen, who are interested in the fields of conservation, wildlife biology, and public speaking. Once a month, we set up discovery stations throughout the San Diego Zoo and discuss one of our four conservation topics: saving species, sustainability, San Diego backyard habitat, and animal care. We meet from nine o'clock to three o'clock, spending the first part of our day participating in workshops, then going out into the zoo to present to the public.

I have been in this program for the past three years, with each session more exciting than the last. Although we don't work directly with the animals, we often get behind-the-scenes interactions with the zookeepers and animals like pangolins [aka scaly anteaters], binturongs [aka bearcat, animal with a face like a cat and a body like a bear], and bonobos [an endangered great ape]. Not at the same time though!

In addition to the rare encounters that we participate in, we also learn valuable skills from the zookeepers about animal care and conservation. This program has helped shape my career goals and inspired me to continue learning about and advocating for animals.

You volunteer at your local humane society. What do you do there and what has that experience taught you?

As a volunteer at the Mary S. Roberts Pet Adoption Center, I socialize the cats and dogs and often work as office liaison in order to help out the staff. I have been volunteering at this center since 2014, with a minimum of six hours a month. As I mentioned before, I have been working to raise money for this shelter since I was eleven, so when I was able to volunteer at the center, I was excited to start working with the animals. I often just sit and read to the cats as a part of socialization. Hearing the voice of someone who cares is a simple comfort shelter animals don't have. It really means a lot to be able to spend time with them and help educate the community about the role they can play to stop animal cruelty. Every time I volunteer there, I learn something new and leave with a greater appreciation for those who spend their time working with and helping these animals.

You are interested in conservation medicine and wildlife biology. Explain what this is about and why it interests you.

Going into high school, I had the intention of becoming a veterinarian that works at a small animal clinic. But as I became more involved with Zoo Corps and other environmental organizations, I began to lean more toward conservation medicine. [Someone who specializes in] conservation medicine takes the practices and skills of a veterinarian and works in the field or in a research facility in order to save species and end extinctions.

I am also very interested in wildlife biology; in order to help animals, we need to fully understand them. I'm excited to dive deeper into this field and begin working alongside those who care as much as I do. One way I will do this is by participating in Cornell University's summer college course, Veterinary Medicine: Conservation Medicine. There, I will spend three weeks doing labs and workshops, listening to lectures, and getting hands-on experience. This course will help prepare me for this field and [give me] a deeper understanding of what it means to work in conservation medicine.

What is your favorite animal?

My favorite animal would have to be Bubba, the pangolin. Pangolins are insectivores that live in Asia and Africa and are most notable for their keratin-based scales. Bubba was confiscated from illegal trade and transferred to the San Diego Zoo, where he now lives. Unfortunately, many pangolins are not as lucky as Bubba and fall prey to the terrible market trade where they poach pangolins for food and false medicinal purposes (which are superstitions throughout many cultures). Bubba is the only known pangolin in captivity in North America and spends his days advocating for the pangolin species and enjoying a delicious concoction of insectivore mix and Ensure. I have met Bubba several times through Zoo Corps and have enjoyed every bit, from the bubbles that foam out of his nose to the amazing life story he has to tell.

What books, magazines, websites, or organizations do you enjoy?

A few times a year, we receive *Living Bird,* a magazine presented by the Cornell Lab of Ornithology, which provides interesting new discoveries in the world of birds. I also enjoy other magazines, such as *Time,* in order to keep up with the world of science and politics. One of my favorite books is *Alexandria of Africa,* a short novel written about a girl who goes to Africa and builds a school for the children of an impoverished village.

And last but not least, one of the organizations I support the most is San Diego Zoo Global. Not only do they advocate for species, but they single-handedly pull them back from the brink of extinction with their world-renowned breeding programs and educational resources. Another organization that I am involved in is GECO, the Green Environment Conservation Organization.

I founded GECO in 2014 as a club on the Martin Luther King High School campus. GECO participates in a host of activities, such as on-campus recycling, nature hikes, and trash cleanups. Every year we host an Environmental Expo in order to showcase what the students have learned throughout the year about conservation and to encourage environmental awareness throughout our community.

Where do you see yourself in ten years?
In five years, I will have graduated from college and be starting to earn my graduate degree for veterinary medicine. In ten years, I will have that degree and be on my way to making a difference in the world, probably working in a clinic or research facility to gain experience before going out into the field. I have not quite made up my mind as to whether I want to work with a private organization such as the San Diego Zoo or with a university. Either way, I know that I will be contributing to the field of conservation and saving the animals I have always loved.

Wildlife Trainers and Educators

Wildlife trainers work in zoos, aquariums, safaris, and circuses—anywhere there are wild animals that need to be trained. To become a wildlife animal trainer, you must be physically fit and patient, with a calm, steady voice and demeanor. You must be willing to repeat, repeat, and repeat again each skill you want the animal to mimic. Training can take months or even years to perfect.

Training wild animals is dangerous work and can result in injury or even death. Plan to work outdoors in every type of weather and during all shifts, including weekends and holidays. If none of this puts you off and you're determined to become a wildlife trainer, then get a bachelor's degree in biology, zoology, or animal science. Get some experience working with large and exotic animals and seek out an apprenticeship with a certified animal trainer.

When Plastic Becomes Bait

In every ocean of the world, there is a dangerous product churning and wreaking havoc with marine life. It is plastic. There is an estimated 250,000 tons of it floating around and it doesn't decompose and disappear. It breaks down into tiny pieces and becomes tempting for sea creatures to consume. But it's not food and the mammals, fish, birds, and turtles that are eating it are starving or slowly being poisoned to death.

Scientists have discovered that besides mistaking the plastic for foods like squid or krill, marine life is being tempted to eat it because of its smell. This is particularly dangerous for tube-nosed seabirds like albatrosses and petrels. These birds fly over the oceans for years searching for food, and only return to land to breed and care for their young. Of the approximately 120 species of tube-nosed seabirds, almost half of them are considered threatened, endangered, or critically endangered.

Tube-nosed birds forage for food wherever they can find it, mainly using their keen sense of smell. It is that habit that started scientists thinking. Could the smell of the plastic be luring the birds to eat it? The answer is yes. Plastic that is left in the ocean for only a few weeks gets coated with algae and begins to give off a sulfur-like scent. That scent is the same as the scent that krill give off when they eat algae. The birds are fooled into thinking that the plastic is food and they eat it.

Types of training can include:

- 🐾 conditioning animals to allow for handling

- 🐾 conditioning animals to tolerate the noise and commotion of an audience

- 🐾 educating people about the animals

- 🐾 encouraging people to support conservation efforts for animals that are endangered in the wild or are losing their native habitats

- 🐾 teaching animals the natural behaviors that will help them survive when returned to the wild

- 🐾 training animals to perform routines

- 🐾 training people to handle animals properly

Quiz: Name That Phobia!

A phobia is an extreme fear of something to the point where it interferes with your life. People can have all kinds of phobias, including acrophobia (a fear of heights), glossophobia (a fear of public speaking), or coulrophobia (a fear of clowns).

Psychologists have given names to many of the animal-specific phobias that people have. Can you guess which animal goes with which phobia? And in case you were wondering, zoophobia is the fear of all animals!

1. Agrizoophobia
  a. Wild animals
  b. Pigeons
  c. Farm animals
  d. Werewolves

2. Ornithophobia
  a. Orcas
  b. Orangutans
  c. Birds
  d. Unicorns

3. Ailurophobia
  a. Basilisks
  b. Cats
  c. Alligators
  d. Snakes

4. Ichthyophobia
  a. Fish
  b. Insects
  c. Yetis
  d. Bears

5. Musophobia
  a. Trolls
  b. Monkeys
  c. Shellfish
  d. Mice

6. Batrachophobia
  a. Bats
  b. Zombies
  c. Amphibians
  d. Rabbits

7. Ophidiophobia
   a. Snakes
   b. Owls
   c. Whales
   d. Chupacabras

8. Cynophobia
   a. Frogs
   b. Dogs
   c. Rats
   d. Cyborgs

9. Helminthophobia
   a. Dinosaurs
   b. Worms
   c. Lions
   d. Moose

10. Selachophobia
   a. Otters
   b. Sloths
   c. Loch Ness Monster
   d. Sharks

Answer Key: 1: a 2: c 3: b 4: a 5: d 6: c 7: a 8: b 9: b 10: d

Raising Farm Animals

Around the world, animals are raised to profit their owners. From alpaca farms in Australia, to ostrich farms in Sweden, to shrimp farms in Belize, to dairy farms in the United States, farmers are working with animals every day. If you are interested in learning about a career working with farm animals, read on!

Farms and Ranches

Farms and ranches are businesses that raise livestock for a variety of purposes. Some keep their animals in barns, pens, or other farm buildings. Others let their animals graze in fenced fields or on vast western prairie lands. The farmers and ranchers care for the animals, protect them from predators, oversee their breeding, and market the animals or the products they produce. Here is a list of some common types of farmers:

- Aquaculture farmers raise fish and shellfish for food or for recreational fishing.

- Cattle farmers raise cows for meat.

Vampire bats don't suck blood; they slurp it up with their tongues. The bats land on the ground and hop along in search of food. The thermoreceptors in their noses help them find flowing blood just under the skin on animals' feet or legs. After they bite, they release a glycoprotein called draculin (named after Count Dracula) in their saliva. Draculin prevents the prey's blood from clotting, thus increasing the flow so the bat can eat more.

- Chicken and turkey farmers raise birds for meat or for eggs.

- Dairy farmers raise cows for milk.

- Exotic animal farmers raise ostriches, llamas, alpacas, buffalo, or elk.

- Goat farmers raise goats for meat, milk, or fiber.

- Horse farmers raise horses for racing, for pets, for rodeos, or for farm work.

- Pig farmers raise pigs for meat.

- Sheep farmers raise sheep for meat or wool.

Farmers and ranchers are small-business owners and need all the skills associated with that, along with the skills needed to care for the animals. Most farmers grow up on a family farm and either inherit it from their parents or start their own farm on nearby land. A farmer's education is usually a high school diploma and on-the-job training. If you didn't grow up on a farm, you will

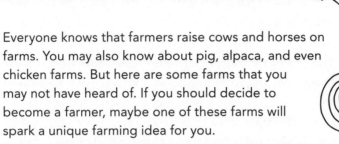

Everyone knows that farmers raise cows and horses on farms. You may also know about pig, alpaca, and even chicken farms. But here are some farms that you may not have heard of. If you should decide to become a farmer, maybe one of these farms will spark a unique farming idea for you.

Armstrong's Cricket Farm in Georgia was started in 1947 by Gene Armstrong, and he became the first commercial cricket grower in the United States. Besides crickets, they also raise and sell worms and nightcrawlers.

Black Ivory Coffee Farm in Bangkok, Thailand, feeds Thai arabica coffee beans to elephants. After the elephants poop out the beans, employees collect, sun-dry, and roast them. These beans are the rarest and most expensive coffee beans is the world, selling for $500 a pound. Coffee made from these beans is world famous and only sold in five-star hotels.

Giraffe Ranch in Tampa, Florida, is a 47-acre working game farm and wildlife preserve where animals have room to roam. As a working ranch, it specializes in exotic species. It is open to the public by reservation and offers safari-style tours through the ranch.

Hartley's Crocodile Adventure Farm in Queensland, Australia, started in 1989, raises crocodiles for their skin and meat. The farm is open to the public and is dedicated to sustainable commercial farming and wildlife and habitat conservation.

Kostroma Moose Farm in Kostroma Oblast, Russia, produces moose milk, which is rich in minerals and used to treat stomach ulcers and other medical conditions. The farm is also a research facility where scientists study moose behavior. The animals roam the forest in the summer and voluntarily return to the farm in the winter, enticed by tasty steamed oats.

need to get some experience working on a farm before you start one of your own.

As farming and ranching become more complex, some are choosing to get more training through government programs like start2farm.gov, or by pursuing a bachelor's degree in agriculture, farm management, or dairy science. All state university systems have at least one land-grant college or university with a school of agriculture. There are a few farms that offer formal apprentice-ship programs, and the federal government has programs like the Beginner Farmer and Rancher Competitive Grants Program, which offers a way for novice farmers to learn from experienced farmers.

Qualities Needed to Be a Farmer or Rancher

- analytical skills to monitor and assess the needs and quality of livestock

- business management skills to keep the farm profitable, prepare budgets, negotiate with banks or creditors, pay employees, negotiate land lease prices, and keep comprehensive animal records

- carpentry and plumbing skills to maintain farm buildings, animal shelters, water lines, and fences

- critical thinking skills to help improve animal care, choose proper food and medicines, and react to unexpected events like disease outbreaks or severe weather events

- interpersonal skills to supervise hired help, sell products and find new markets, and negotiate with vendors like feed stores or hay sellers

- mechanical skills to maintain and operate machinery

When it comes to the usefulness of all parts of a slaughtered animal, none can compare with the pig. In 2015, British writer and researcher Christein Meindertsma decided to follow a pig from its slaughter to the end consumer. That pig became part of a whopping 185 different products! Besides meat, here are ten of the more interesting ones:

- bread (protein in pig hair softens it)
- candles and crayons (fatty acids from bone fat stiffen the wax)
- dog treats (ears and noses become snacks)
- energy bars (collagen is a cheap protein)
- fruit juice (gelatin absorbs cloudy elements)
- licorice and chewing gum (gelatin creates texture)
- paint brushes (hair becomes bristles)
- tambourines (bladders become drum skins)
- yogurt (calcium from bones fortifies the yogurt)

Farm or Ranch Managers

Farm and ranch managers oversee a farm or ranch that raises animals for food, products, or competition. They are involved in every stage of an animal's life, from breeding to final slaughter or sale. They also purchase equipment and supplies, maintain buildings and pasture lands, make sure that the farm complies with government regulations, and hire, train and manage other farm workers.

Managers spend most of their time outside, in all weather conditions. They must be physically fit and able to manage dangerous animals. The hours can be long, especially during the spring calving, lambing, or foaling season. Livestock need care year-round, including nights, weekends, and holidays. Working your way up to ranch manager doesn't require a formal education. You get there through hard work and a reputation for being good at your job. The best place to start is as a ranch hand.

Some ranch manager duties include:

- analyzing productivity and offering ways to improve

- buying and selling animals

- managing employees, including hiring, training, scheduling, and firing

- negotiating prices for livestock and supplies

- projecting budgets based on changing markets

- promoting the farm's brand or products

- tracking expenses and preparing budgets

- writing grants or business proposals to help find capital

- understanding the meat or product markets

TOP DOG *profile*

Name: Casey L. Aschim
Job: Farm Manager at Larry Pekkola and Son

When did you first become interested in working with animals and decide to make it the focus of your career?

In middle school, when I began showing market lambs and steers in 4-H and eventually FFA. I enjoyed caring for the animals and eventually selling them at the youth auction. It was very exciting to have a project of my own that I could make some money with at a young age. As I have become older, I really enjoy commercial cattle and hogs and devote my time to these species.

What education/work path did you take to get to your current position?

Being involved in FFA through high school and working on my family farm, I knew I wanted to pursue a career in agriculture. Not necessarily on the farm, but in the industry. I decided to attend an agricultural-based community college that had direct affiliation with my local state university so my credits would transfer easily. I graduated with a bachelor of science degree in agriculture business management with a minor in general agriculture. In college, I took various beef and pork production classes and lots of business management classes to maximize the return and efficiency of our cow herd at home, as well as our crop production.

Explain the life cycle of your cattle herd.

The cattle stay around our farm for various periods of time, depending on what they are. Cows are female cattle that have had a calf at least once. They may live on the farm for ten years or more. This depends on their health, whether or not they are having good-quality calves, how much milk they produce for the calf, as well as their conformation and disposition.

Bulls are the "daddy" cattle. They usually average three to five years on the farm, depending on if we need to keep any of their daughters to replace older cows. We will take the bulls to auction when they are done breeding so they can be sold to another producer or used for meat.

After the cows and bulls breed, a calf develops and is born in nine months, similar to a human baby's gestational period. When male calves are born, the testes are banded to prevent them from becoming bulls, which produce inadequate meat when they become mature due to too much testosterone. These castrated males, called steers, will be with their mothers for about eight to nine months, eating grass and drinking milk the whole time.

The female calves are called heifers. They will take the place of old cows or cows that have reproductive issues. Any heifers that aren't used as "replacement heifers" will be fed up to butcher size just like the steers.

In the last month, all the calves are separated and weaned from their moms. They will continue to eat grass, light amounts of grain, and grass hay so they can gain weight and reach a nice butcher size. To reach an ideal butcher size of 1,200 to 1,400 pounds, they receive lots of protein-packed grain to fatten them up in the final three months and are butchered at about eighteen months old.

This is the system for my farm, but there are many facets of cattle production that you can get involved in. Maybe you want to just raise breeding bulls or replacement heifers. A lot of producers have cow/calf operations and sell the young calves to feedlots at a weaning age. Other producers buy these calves and put them in their feedlots to fatten them up to butcher sizes. The options for how you can raise beef are limitless, depending on which area most interests you.

How do you handle the cattle? Are there any special things you do?
When handling cattle, the key is to be calm, quiet, and collected. Cattle don't like loud noises or flashy movements. So, if you are composed, they will keep their composure. Also, cattle are herd animals, so it is important to always keep at least two animals together. When trying to push cattle into a trailer or squeeze chute, it is best to stay close to the rear of the animal so they sense your touch rather than be a few feet behind where they can kick you. If you stay close, they think you're another animal, and it calms them better. If you do have an animal that gets riled up, it's better to let them be for a bit so they can calm down. If you keep pushing them, there is a good chance they will go over, through,

or around whatever barrier you have that keeps them contained. Then you have a real problem on your hands.

Besides raising cattle, what are some of the other responsibilities of a farm manager?

Managing a farm requires many skills besides taking care of livestock. We grow a lot of crops, so we have to be on tractors in the fall and spring preparing the ground for planting. Once the crops are planted, they need constant attention. They require fertilizer to grow; chemicals to manage weeds, pests and diseases; and eventually, in the summertime, they need to be harvested.

Once harvested, the crops go to a processor that cleans impurities like weed seeds, broken seeds, and chaff out of the seeds. After being cleaned, the seeds are put into bags and onto pallets so they can be shipped all over the country and world. Some of these crops, like corn, oats, wheat, and barley, are used to feed cattle and other species of animals.

On our farm, we mainly feed the broken and off-quality seeds that are separated off at the cleaner because they are a cheap by-product of the crops and it leaves more of the pure seed for us to sell into other markets. These feed grains are put through a rolling mill or grinder to make the feed more palatable for the animals, and they are also able to get more nutrients from the processed feed.

Besides crop production, as a farm manager I am in the shop being a mechanic, I'm going to meetings to learn about new technologies for enhanced farming, and I spend quite a bit of time in the office budgeting, invoicing, and just making sure the business runs smoothly.

What do you enjoy most and least about working on a farm?

My favorite part of being a farm manager is the variety of work you get to do. One day I may be on a tractor, the next day I am moving cattle to new pastures, and the following day I am at the desk making invoices for the cattle or crops I've sold. It's wonderful working a job that never gets boring, even working countless hours.

In turn, the long hours in the summer start to wear on you a bit, but the part I dislike most about farming is you can do everything right all year round, and when harvest rolls around you can get an untimely rain or storm and your year of hard work gets diminished by mother nature. That is part of the risk of farming; it's not for the faint of heart.

What tips would you give kids who are interested in pursuing a career as a farm manager?
If you're interested in becoming a farm manager, I would recommend you get a job on a farm. Most farmers will be happy to hire you as a high schooler if you have an interest in farming. This will give you a feel for what is required on a farm and the long hours involved in farming. If you're able to stand the long hours, dust, dirt, and heat, and still enjoy it at the end of the day, then you may have the heart of a farmer. At that point, you should plan to go to college, and plan to get a degree in agriculture, business, animal science, or another similar field to gain the extra skills needed to manage a farm. You should also know that a farm manager's salary is good, but if you are more money driven, this is not the career for you, although it will provide a great lifestyle.

What is your favorite animal and why?
Even though I predominantly raise cattle on my farm, my favorite animals are pigs. I love their excited personalities, and they are a lot of fun to watch interact with their buddies in the pen. That being said, there is nothing better than watching a week-old calf being turned out on lush spring pasture with his mother.

||||||||||||||||||||||||||||||||||||||||||||||||||||||||||||||||||||||||||||||||||||||||||||||||||||||||

Cowboys, Cowgirls, and Wranglers
Today, most cowboys and wranglers work on large ranches where they raise huge herds of animals for slaughter or on ranches that

The American cowboy is a legendary figure, made famous through stories told in movies, on television, and in the pages of books. Here are a few things you may not know about the life of a cowboy in the Old West:

- ❖ They lived in bunkhouses with lots of other cowboys.

- ❖ Their average pay was around twenty-five to forty dollars a month.

- ❖ The harmonica was their favorite instrument.

- ❖ They sang songs at night to soothe the cattle.

- ❖ They wore their clothes for weeks at a time without changing.

- ❖ "Cookie," the camp cook, was the most important person in camp.

- ❖ Eight to twelve cowboys could move three thousand head of cattle at a pace of fifteen miles a day.

- ❖ Many cowboys were former Civil War soldiers, and about a quarter of them were former slaves.

offer tourists an old-fashioned ranch experience. They dress the same as they have for over 150 years, in attire that is perfect for the work: chaps to protect their legs, cowboy hats to protect their eyes, and jeans, boots, gloves, and bandannas.

To become a cowboy, all you need is a love of the outdoors, a strong body, and the ability to ride a horse. Some cowboys have second jobs working for rodeos or circuses as livestock handlers. They may work with bulls in rodeos, train horses for the circus, or focus on the safety of the animals and the audiences.

Cowboy and wrangler duties include:

- assisting hurt, pregnant, or birthing animals
- caring for and maintaining saddles and tack
- cleaning and maintaining stalls and barns
- cutting firewood
- feeding, watering, and branding livestock
- guiding guests on horseback rides
- hosting and entertaining guests
- maintaining trails
- monitoring and repairing fences
- moving livestock to different pastures
- repairing equipment
- protecting animals from predators

Although men dominate the field, women are still in the picture. From the time the West was first settled to today, women have worked alongside men, caring for animals, performing in rodeos, and riding the range.

Alyssa Barnes is a cowgirl with a website and blog called *Earn Your Spurs*. She understands the cowgirl/cowboy lifestyle and offers five truths for you to ponder before deciding that this is the career for you:

1. **You're Going to Get Dirty.** Being a cowboy, regardless of the variety, is not a clean job. First of all, it's outside, so you have actual dirt to contend with, but that's not all. Animals are dirty. Poop, snot, mud, eye boogers, pus, blood, saliva . . . at any given time one to many of these substances will likely be present on a horse or a cow or a dog or whatever other animal you are contending with. . . . Wherever you get your "cowboy training," be prepared to wear your filth like a badge of honor.

2. **Cows Are Not Cuddly.** Some horses can be kind of cuddly, but they are also big and fast and can hurt you without even meaning to. That is why it is really important to understand their behavior, know how to approach them, and how to stay out of their way. But if you think horses are bad, cows are hardly ever cuddly. . . . If you get them cornered in a confined space and you happen to be in the wrong spot, they will kick you. . . . Bulls aren't much different. . . . They don't even need an excuse to come after you.

3. **Your Skin Needs to Be Thick.** Cowboys aren't big on sugarcoating. They tend to tell it like it is. It's actually an admirable quality when you think about it. You don't ever have to guess where you stand with a cowboy. If he feels you are impacting him in a negative way or impeding his progress, he is going to let you know.

4. **Assume You Know Nothing.** Even if you think you know something already, it never hurts to hear it again. Often, listening to someone else explain it, perhaps in a different way, helps it to sink in. Ask questions when you don't understand something. Plus, everyone does things a

little bit differently. Being a know-it-all doesn't make you seem smart. It just makes you look foolish when you do something wrong that you supposedly already knew how to do.

5. **Be Prepared to "Rub Some Dirt on It."** In the cowboy line of work, getting injured at some point is likely. Could be a broken finger, rope burn, or just your bruised pride. But here's the thing. Cowboys are tough. . . . If you get kicked in the shin by a wily little calf, it is likely going to hurt and probably leave a bruise, but you might want to keep it to yourself. Either that, or be prepared to be teased and taunted unmercifully for acting like a "little girl."[1]

> Located in Fort Worth, Texas, the National Cowgirl Museum and Hall of Fame is the only museum of its kind, dedicated to "honoring and celebrating women . . . whose lives exemplify the courage, resilience, and independence that shape the American West."[2] Today, the museum archives hold over four thousand artifacts and information about more than 750 remarkable women.

Animal Reproduction and Breeding

From a person breeding a dog to sell her puppies, to ranchers breeding cattle for leaner meat, to the US Fish and Wildlife Service breeding the California condor to keep it from going extinct, people around the world breed animals for many reasons. Here are a few of them:

🐾 To enhance physical characteristics. A labradoodle is a cross between a Labrador retriever and a poodle. The goal is to get puppies that are gentle and easily trained like a

Labrador, but have the easy-care, low-shedding coat of a poodle.

- ❖ To increase production. Dairy cows or fiber goats are selectively bred to increase the amount of milk they produce or enhance the quality of their fiber.

- ❖ To change body mass. Beef cattle are crossbred to create larger animals, or animals that have leaner meat.

- ❖ To increase offspring rates. Pigs are bred to increase the number of piglets born to a sow. Chickens are bred to encourage those that produce more eggs over a longer egg-laying lifespan.

- ❖ To prevent extinction. Animals are bred in captivity and their offspring are released into the wild. This is done to boost the numbers in wild populations and promote healthy genetic diversity.

Breeding managers have a bachelor's degree in reproductive physiology. They work on large farms or at breeding facilities. The job entails monitoring animal reproductive cycles, deciding which animals to breed based on a desired outcome, and maintaining detailed records so that good outcomes can be repeated.

Reproductive physiologists have at least a master's degree. They work for animal research companies, pharmaceutical companies, animal health organizations, or universities. They study genetics, statistics, computer science, and molecular genetics. They can teach at the college level, work on research projects, and publish articles in animal science journals.

Some reproductive physiologists conduct research to improve treatments for animals with reproductive disorders. They study disease-causing organisms, help create new medications, perform tests, and sometimes conduct large-scale research projects.

SPOTLIGHT

Robert Bakewell (1725–1795), First Scientific Breeder

Robert Bakewell was born in 1725 in Dishley, England, the only surviving son of a tenant farmer who was known to be "one of the most ingenious and able farmers of his neighbourhood."[3] Bakewell's father encouraged him to learn as much as possible about the animals he tended. To that end, he encouraged Bakewell to travel throughout England, Ireland, and Holland, gathering information on all the newest animal treatments and practices of the day.

As a young man, Bakewell worked as an apprentice for his father on a 450-acre (178-hectare) farm that for generations had pushed the boundaries of new farming methods. When Bakewell inherited it, the farm already had a reputation for being a model for others to copy. He continued that tradition by becoming a pioneer in grassland irrigation, taking sections of land and testing different ways to water and fertilize the plants. He even diverted rivers and built canals to flood the fields in order to get them watered the way he wanted.

Bakewell's greatest innovation came when he decided to control the breeding of his animals. At the time, males and females grazed together, mating and randomly creating different breeds and characteristics. He decided to separate the males from the females and only allow mating that was deliberate and for a specific reason. By doing this, he could breed out unwanted traits and promote the traits he wanted. He started with an old breed of sheep. Through selective breeding, he developed a new breed that was bigger, had a great fleece, and had very fat upper legs and shoulders (a cut of meat that was extremely popular). He also hired out his rams to other farmers to help them improve the quality of their herds.

When it came to cows, Bakewell noticed that longhorns ate less but put on weight faster than other breeds. Through selective breeding, he encouraged the longhorns' growth rate while maintaining a cow that was fat and meaty too. He also selectively bred many pigs and horses. Although some of Bakewell's methods and outcomes stirred up controversy during his lifetime, many of his practices are commonly used today. Bakewell died in 1795 at the age of seventy.

Other Jobs Working with Farm Animals

Farriers oversee the care, maintenance, and shoeing of horses' hooves. There are horseshoeing schools across the nation where you can earn certificates, or you can learn through an apprenticeship with an experienced farrier who is willing to teach you the trade.

Petting zoos exist across the United States, in every state. They can be found in larger zoos, parks, carnivals, and fairs. Some are small and have a handful of animals, while others are larger and have lots of animals, including some exotics like llamas, wallabies, and potbellied pigs. Some petting zoos travel from event to event, especially during the summer months. Petting zoos feature animals that are gentle enough for children to pet and feed. Working for a petting zoo doesn't require any special education, and most train their employees in basic animal care.

Shearers remove the coats from sheep, goats, or alpacas and pack the fiber to send to market. Most shearers work outdoors and can work alone or for shearing companies. They shear in the United States in the spring and then travel to other countries like Australia and New Zealand in the winter. Shearing is hard work, and a typical day can last from sunup to sundown. The herd of sheep to be sheared can range in size from one hundred to over ten thousand heads, but a professional shearer can shear a sheep in under two minutes. To find training, you need to work as an apprentice or look for university extension classes.

Raise Your Own Chickens

From barnyards to backyards, people across the country are raising chickens for their eggs. To raise your own chicken, you will need permission and help from a parent. It may take some persuasion, a promise to do the work, and some cute smiles and hugs. Once you get a yes, here are some guidelines to get you started.

Make an Informed Decision
Before you buy your first chick, make sure you're ready for responsible chicken ownership. Chickens stop laying eggs years before they die of old age at seven or eight. That means you will have to care for your chicken for years after she stops laying, or you will have to butcher her. Responsible owners decide what they will do when their chickens become sick, old, or no longer productive. With the help of your parents,

92

decide before you get your chick what the end of her life will look like.

If you live in the city, check your town's zoning ordinances to see if you're allowed to raise chickens. Many cities allow backyard chickens but limit the number you're allowed to raise. Because chickens are social animals, it's best to raise at least two. Remember, when you buy a chicken, there is a slight chance that you will get a rooster. Many cities don't allow roosters because they like to crow a lot. What will you do with your chick if it grows up to be a rooster?

Decide the Breed of Your Chicken

Take your time and do your chicken research. There are tons of books to buy or borrow from the library. There are also websites like LivestockConservancy.org, ModernFarmer.com, and MyPetChicken.com that offer guides on choosing the perfect breed for you.

Hatchlings

You have three options for buying your first chickens: fertile eggs, day-old chicks, or pullets. Fertile eggs require an incubator and careful attention until they hatch. Pullets are 16- to 26-week-old birds that are almost ready to start laying eggs. For this activity, we're going to focus on the most common option, day-old chicks.

Purchase day-old chicks from a farm store, hatchery, or co-op. Make sure you specify that you only want hens, not roosters. Healthy chicks are bright-eyed and active with fluffy, soft down. When your chicks come home, they'll need a "brooder" box. Here's what you will need to build one:

- plastic storage box

- wood shavings or shredded paper for bedding

- heat lamp

- thermometer

- waterer

- feeder

- chick starter feed

Line the bottom of the storage box with at least two inches of bedding. Position the heat lamp so that it shines down and is at least a foot above the top of the bedding. Place your thermometer under the light. Chicks do best when the floor temperature is ninety to ninety-five degrees Fahrenheit (thirty-two to thirty-five degrees Celsius).

Put your chicks in the brooder along with the waterer and feeder. Check these each day and keep them full and clean. When you first put your chicks in the brooder, dip their beaks in the water and the feeder so they know where they are.

If your chicks lie flat on the floor with their wings spread out, the brooder is too hot. If they are cuddled together under the light, your brooder is too cold. When the temperature is just right, your chicks should be walking around, eating, interacting with each other, and napping comfortably.

Pick up your chicks for at least five minutes every day. This will help them become more comfortable around humans. As your chicks grow, they will lose their down and grow feathers. They will also need more room. Plan to move your chicks into bigger and bigger areas as they grow.

Fledglings
After about six to eight weeks, if the outside air stays above fifty degrees, your chicks are ready to move into their coop. There are many options for building or buying a coop. Here are some important things to remember:

❧ Chickens need three to four square feet of living space each. When planning your coop, design it with a door so you can easily clean it. It also needs good natural lighting and ventilation but should protect the birds from harsh weather and predators.

❧ Chickens instinctively want to perch somewhere when they sleep. Each chicken needs a 10- to 12-inch section of roosting space. A 1- to 1 1/2–inch diameter pole or tree limb will work.

❧ You need at least one nesting box, about a foot square and four inches deep, for every four hens. Put in enough padding to keep the eggs from cracking.

Thoroughly clean your coop at least once a year. Wear a dust mask and scrub everything with bleach and hot water, and then wait for the coop to dry before replacing the bedding.

Hens

Once you've built your coop and have healthy adult chickens, your job isn't over! Check on them regularly, collect the eggs, and make sure they have plenty of water, food, grit, and calcium.

Layer hens generally lay two eggs every three days from the time they're six months old, with breaks during molting season. During the winter, they may lay fewer eggs or even stop laying. By hooking up a lightbulb to the coop and providing them with at least fourteen hours of light each day, you can increase egg production in the winter.

Chickens can be fenced in or free-range. Fences should be at least four feet high and made from wire mesh to keep the birds in and predators out.

Enjoy your birds! There's nothing sweeter than seeing a happy flock of chickens, pecking away at bugs and basking in the sunshine.

‖‖‖

Name: Dustin Talbott
Age: 14
Job (when not studying!): Rodeo
Rider and Future Rancher

What were your early experiences with animals?

I was pretty much raised on a horse. I remember going to a lot of barrel races to watch my mom compete. I started competing in rodeo when I was three years old. I competed at barrel races. I had play days on my ponies and horses. I also went on many, many trail rides and rode in parades.

This will be my fifth year participating in 4-H. I have raised a market hog these last four years and will be raising another one this year, along with showing two Maine-Anjou (MA) heifers. As an eighth grader in FFA, I have competed in photography, proficiency judging, and veterinary science knowledge. I have done community service work too. In the future, I would like to do agriculture mechanics welding and agriculture vehicle mechanics.

You are raising a heifer to show. Describe her and your experiences working with her.

She is a Maine-Anjou heifer who is a yearling. Her official name is LT Tundra Steppin in Faith, aka "Destiny." Destiny tends to be quite stubborn and opinionated. I have to groom her, which includes washing her, loading her into a grooming chute, blowing her out with a cattle blower, and brushing her with a cattle brush/comb. I walk her and practice setting her up for show, mainly getting her to place her feet in the correct position. I feed her a certain amount of hay and grain each day to make sure she is gaining weight or maintaining her weight.

I am planning to breed her this spring, so I have had to research different bulls to find a good match so I get a good-quality calf. I really enjoy looking at different bulls to crossbreed with. I plan to show her this year in Roseburg, Oregon, and in Canby, Oregon, and also at the fair. There might be a few more shows that we go to also. She will be the start of my breeding herd, which will include purebred Maine-Anjou and club calves [calves raised for show at competition events like state and county fairs]. My plan is to breed and sell club calves. Eventually I hope to use the money I get from these to help pay for my college, buy more cows or calves with good bloodlines to improve and grow my herd, and maybe one day have a commercial herd.

Describe your experiences in the rodeo.

I participate in team roping as a "header," breakaway roping, calf tying, and chute dogging. I compete in the Northwest Youth Rodeo Association (NYRA) and a few other rodeos in Washington and Oregon. With NYRA, I participate in many rodeos from June through August. I have made many, many memories through rodeo.

What organizations do you enjoy?

SullivanSupply.com, AQHA (American Quarter Horse Association), AMAA (American Maine Anjou Association), and the NRA (National Rifle Association).

What do you like to do in your spare time?

When I have spare time, I like to try and hang out with friends, shoot guns, hunt, snowboard, and spend time with my family.

Where do you see yourself in ten years?

Graduated from college and hopefully having a good-paying job/ career. Also I would like to still have my cattle herd, and maybe be living in central or eastern Oregon.

6

Tending Bugs, Birds, and Fishes

Birds, bugs, and fishes aren't the first creatures one thinks of when discussing careers working with animals, but they are incredibly important. Birds spread seeds, eat pesky bugs, and fill our skies with beauty. Bugs spread pollen and are food for other bugs, birds, and reptiles. And fish are a source of food for animals higher up the food chain, including us. If you are interested in working with insects, birds, or fish, then maybe there's a career in this chapter for you.

Just like snakes, tarantulas molt as they grow, a process that can take from fifteen minutes to several hours. When the tarantula molts, it sheds not only its skin, but also its fangs, stomach lining, hair, spinners, and reproductive organs—which are all replaced with new ones! If a tarantula loses a leg it, too, regenerates during a molt. Tarantulas also have two retractable claws on each leg that they use for climbing, just like a cat. How cool is that?!

Bugs

Bugs are incredibly important to the health of the earth's ecosystems. By "bug," we mean the approximately nine out of ten species of animals that inhabit this planet. Granted, there are a few irritating bugs in the mix—the ones that bite, sting, eat our food, and spread diseases. But the vast majority of bugs are harmless and helpful. The good ones eat other insects, help break down dead vegetation, spread pollen, make things like honey and silk, and are food for other creatures, including many people around the world.

Apiarists, or Beekeepers

An apiarist raises bees for honey, beeswax, and crop pollination. Most beekeepers are self-taught or learn through an unofficial apprenticeship with a local beekeeper. To work with bees, you should first ensure that you aren't allergic to them, aren't afraid of being stung, and love to work outdoors. To start your own hives, look for books, classes, workshops, or conferences where you can learn the essentials:

- bee diseases and treatments

- bee reproduction and behaviors

- building and maintaining hives

- collecting, packaging, and marketing honey, beeswax, and pollen

- how to handle bees

- keeping accurate records of the colonies and production levels

- plant bloom cycles and pollen quality

Most beekeepers work for themselves, marketing and selling their honey and other products. Some work for large companies that have huge factories that produce and sell mass-market honey. And some work for horticultural or seed crop companies managing the hives that pollinate the fields.

|||||||||||||||||||||||||||||||||||||||||||||||||||||||||||||||||||||||||||||||||||||||||||||||||||||||||||||||||||||||||||||||||

Name: Benjamin Pierce Oppenheimer
Age: 10
Job (when not studying!): Beekeeper

When did you first discover your love for bees and decide that you wanted to work with them?
When I was eight I planted sunflowers. They grew until their centers were full of big seeds. When I went to harvest the seeds, the seed shells were empty! There was nothing inside the seed shells because there were no pollinators. I researched pollination, found out about bees, and became hooked on bees.

Tell us about your bees.
Bees are interesting and fun. They make advanced colonies, survive on two different foods (pollen and honey), and they communicate with each other by dancing. I started with one hive of ten thousand bees and they grew to about forty thousand. I keep my hive in my backyard where my family and I sit and watch the bees at work. My bees have never swarmed. They only do that if there are pesticides, temperature problems in the hive, too many mites or bugs, and stuff like that. We have green lizards in the yard

that eat the hive beetles. I do not use any poisons in or near my hive. I would much rather not. Sometimes I pet my bees. They are super soft, like a fuzzy dead leaf. Most of my friends are okay with the bees, but some get nervous.

I set up my hive by getting a nuc [nucleus colony, a small honeybee colony created from a larger colony] that held one queen and a bunch of workers. Then I transferred those bees to a wooden box that I had painted yellow. I added more levels of boxes (supers) and frames inside each box when the bees needed more space. I knew they needed more space because they would hang out in front of the hive entrance.

I use the smoker to inspect the hive and get honey. I light it myself. Sometimes my brother or mom helps me lift out the frames because the honey makes them heavy. The hardest part is seeing dead bees in front of my hive. Bees only live two weeks, except for the queen.

Have you ever been stung?
Yes, but I don't really count the number of times I have been stung. It feels bad, but the worst part is when the stings puff up and itch. A funny story was when a bee crawled into my big brother's armpit but did not sting him. My brother used to be afraid of bees. Now he isn't.

When we bought my hive, they got loose in my mom's car. They were crawling everywhere and we had to drive an hour with them loose in the car. No stings. When we went through a drive-through line, the people in the car behind us honked and screamed to tell us, "THERE ARE BEES IN YOUR CAR!" They thought we did not know this and that the bees were dangerous.

How much honey and wax do you get and what do you do with it?
When I want to get the honey, I remove the honey frames after I puff smoke on the bees. The smoker calms them down. (The smoker is a fire in a can that puffs smoke directly into the hive

and slightly irritates the bees.) Once I remove the frames, I brush the bees off the frames with a soft brush. Next, I take the frames inside, slice off the coating of wax, and watch the honey drip out into my bucket.

I crush the wax to get the rest of the honey out and let it sit in a mesh filter so the honey can drip out into the bottom of my bucket. I wait a day for all the honey to drain through the filter. Then I collect the honey in bottles and sell it. I have a label that I put on the bottles. I paid my brother twenty-five dollars to design my label on the computer. I get a lot of honey. I sell it, but I never have enough for all the customers. [Benjamin's honey won an award at the University of Florida's Bee College honey show. He was the youngest person to ever win an award!]

I save the wax and use it later. I make candles and lip balm with it. Soon I will use the balm to mix in the herbal things I am learning how to make out of aloe, mint, cherry blossoms, and lavender. In the future, I plan to keep multiple hives and start breeding bees for better traits. An example of these traits would be faster honey production.

President Obama mailed me some honey from the White House beehive and sent me seeds and a letter. I wrote him a letter about his plan to plant wildflowers alongside federal highways. Last month, he invited me to the White House. I saw his beehive. It was amazing.

Where do you see yourself in the future?
My next project will be about bumblebees. Then, I want to volunteer for the Florida Wildlife Sanctuary. In ten years, I see myself in Oregon breeding bees. I want to go to Cornell University because of its biology departments.

||||||||||||||||||||||||||||||||||||||||||||||||||||||||||||||||||||||||||||||||||||||||||||||||||||||||||||||||||||||||||||||

Pest Control Workers or Exterminators
Pest control workers are on the front line of managing unwanted insects in homes, businesses, and agricultural fields. They are

also responsible for killing insects like the mosquito, which carries diseases like malaria or the Zika virus. Workers spread chemicals designed to kill unwanted pests. They work for large agribusinesses, all levels of government, small businesses, and as independent consultants. Most workers get on-the-job training. Because you will work with harsh chemicals, all states require that you be licensed. Some states also require that you have a high school degree, pass a background check, and/or complete an internship.

TOP DOG profile

Name: Kristie Reddick and Jessica Honaker
Job: Entomologists, the Bug Chicks

When did you first become interested in bugs and decide to make them the focus of your career?

Kristie: When I was growing up, I was a dancer and actor. I spent all of my time performing or rehearsing. But I had always loved animals. In eighth grade, I wanted to get into a high-level marine biology course because I was nuts about whales, but my teacher told me I had no aptitude for science. She told me I was good on stage and that's what I should do.

Jess: As a kid, I played sports a lot and was in and out of physical therapy for various sprains and strains I would acquire during the season. No matter what my injury was, the PTs were always there to aid my recovery. The idea of having such a positive impact on people really resonated with me, and so I began to concentrate on physical therapy as a career.

What education/work path did you take to get to where you are today?

Kristie: I got my BFA in theater and was performing, but I felt like I had missed something. I went back to school for a second bachelor's degree and traveled to Africa to study large mammals, which was my secret dream since the age of five. I took one entomology class with an amazing teacher and the whole world opened up for me. I call it "putting on my small eyes." The bugs in Kenya won me over, and it's where I first saw a solifuge [an arachnid also called a camel spider or sun spider]. I determined then and there that I would study them in East Africa. Now I have my master of science in entomology and wrote my thesis on the solifuges of Kenya. The little voice inside your head? You should always listen to it. Don't ever let someone tell you what you are capable of or who you should be.

Jess: While in undergrad, I had to take an invertebrate zoology class and it changed the way I thought about the world. Between the content of the class and the enthusiasm of my incredible professor, my career course was altered forever. I began to see how important insects and other arthropods are to the healthy function of our planet, and how they affect every single facet of our lives (even if we don't realize it). After getting my master of science in entomology, I'm able to positively impact people in a different way—through education and conservation.

Kristie: We were both really lucky to be inspired by great teachers. A passionate teacher can change your life in ways you can't imagine! Jess was originally studying to be a physical therapist and I went to university for theater, but now it's all about the bugs and we've never looked back.

What is it about bugs that fascinates you so much?

Arthropods (animals with exoskeletons and jointed appendages) are the most numerous and diverse animals on the planet! They have an incredible effect on the planet, from pollinating

70 percent of our food to soil decomposition for all of the forests. We need them! Also, there are so many of them that we will never run out of species to learn about.

You have an awesome website, TheBugChicks.com. Why did you start it and what do you hope to achieve with it?
We started our website in 2011. We wanted a place for people to learn about arthropods in a fun, accurate way. Eventually we hope it will be a destination site for lots of people and for junior entomologists!

As small-business owners and media personalities, what is the hardest part of maintaining this career?
Wow. Balancing time between content creation, creative projects, and business management is really hard. We do everything ourselves. But as we grow, we will be hiring people to help us. If you grow up to run a small business it's all about delegation!

The easiest or most fun part?
We LOVE making videos and dreaming up ways to teach a hard concept. We make all of the costumes. It's stressful to film ourselves, but it is so much fun. Often it involves traveling to interesting places. We love to be together making insect science fun!

What are some of the projects you are currently working on?
Right now we are busy pitching books and a TV show about arthropods! We think women should be on TV talking about nature and not competing with each other. We need positive female role models in the media and STEM [science, technology, engineering, and mathematics].

What tips can you give students who are thinking about becoming entomologists?
Study hard in science and math. It's important to be a good writer too, because scientists need to be able to communicate with people

who are not scientists. Also, when you learn about insects on the internet, make sure you're on a good website that ends in .edu or .gov, or you can go to our site!

Describe your favorite bug or your favorite bug story.
Our whole time filming in Costa Rica for some insect videos was pretty amazing. We filmed bullet ants and spiny katydids and went out into the forest every night to find incredible arthropods and snakes and frogs and sloths. It was a dream come true. Plus, we got to see a giant elephant beetle the size of a softball!

Birds

Birds are important because they help keep all the earth's ecosystems in balance. They eat pesky insects (especially the ones that eat crops and trees), pollinate plants and scatter seeds (mainly by eating them and then pooping them out somewhere else), feed on dead animals, and slow the spread of diseases by eating the insects that carry them.

Birds are the watchmen that help monitor the health of an area. Have you heard the phrase "canary in a coalmine"? Like the canaries that warned miners when there were dangerous gases in the mine, all birds warn those who will listen that an ecosystem is in danger. If the birds are disappearing, something is wrong, and someone needs to do something to help. Maybe that someone will be you?

Some of the careers listed in other chapters of this book can focus on working with birds. Veterinarians can treat exotic birds like parrots or canaries, or domestic birds like chickens or ducks. Ranchers can build their businesses around raising ostriches or emus. And there are aviary zookeepers who work with birds in bird exhibits. They care for a variety of species, from flamingos to wild song birds.

They also work with other animals within their exhibits, like fish or turtles in the water features. They are responsible for the birds' daily needs, including feeding them and maintaining their habitat. They watch for health problems and changes in behavior, and keep detailed records of each bird. They train interns, interact with zoo visitors, and participate in zoo programs. This job requires at least a two-year degree in an animal-related program like zoology or zoo animal technology.

In the late 1800s, worry about declining bird populations inspired Frank M. Chapman, a member of the newly formed Audubon Society, to propose a new holiday, the Christmas Bird Count, where people count birds rather than hunt them. The first year, twenty-five groups of bird watchers counted ninety different species from Toronto, Canada, to the northeastern United States. Today, from mid-December through early January, thousands of volunteers participate. The data they gather helps guide conservation efforts across North America.

 # SPOTLIGHT

John James Audubon (1785–1851), American Ornithologist and Wildlife Artist

Jean Rabin was born on April 26, 1785, in Saint Domingue, part of a Caribbean island that today is called Haiti. His father was a French sea captain and plantation owner, and his mother was Captain Audubon's Creole servant, Jeanne Rabin. She died while Jean was still a baby. When Jean was six, he and his half-sister went to France to live with their father and stepmother. At the age of nine, his father legally adopted both children and changed Jean's name to Jean-Jacques Fougère Audubon.

When Audubon was eighteen, war broke out between England and France. To keep him from him from being forced to serve in Emperor Napoleon Bonaparte's army, his father sent him to America to live on the family's estate outside Philadelphia. Before arriving in America, Jean-Jacques changed his name to John James Audubon.

While living at the estate, he enjoyed hunting, drawing, and music. The estate was also where his interest in birds developed and flourished. He was the first to study the migration of the eastern phoebe. By tying strings to their legs, he learned that the birds returned to the same nesting sites each year. He spent much of his free time drawing pictures of every bird he saw.

Audubon married Lucy Bakewell, and when the family estate failed he moved to Louisville, Kentucky, and opened a general store. When business slowed, they packed up and moved further west into the unsettled territory of Henderson, Kentucky. He opened another store that flourished for a while. But when hard times hit again in 1819, he was sent to jail for unpaid debts.

After his time in jail, feeling uncertain about his future, Audubon decided to pursue his love for observing and drawing birds. He and his family traveled south and settled in New Orleans, where he perfected his artistic skills by painting portraits and teaching others how to draw. Along the way, he built up a huge portfolio of bird drawings that were immensely popular because of their perfect, lifelike representation of each bird.

In 1826, Audubon took his work to England and was an overnight success. His bird portraits and his dramatic descriptions of wilderness life, which took over fourteen years to complete, enthralled the public. While there, he published his famous *Birds of America* book and then collaborated with Scottish ornithologist William MacGillivray on the *Ornithological Biographies*, a collection of life histories of each bird in the *Birds of America* book.

Audubon's work earned him a good living and well-deserved fame. After returning to the United States, he traveled around the country in search of birds and finally settled in New York City. His last book, *Viviparous Quadrupeds of North America*, was a work devoted to mammals. Audubon suffered from senility in his last years of life, so his son finished the illustrations and his longtime friend, John Bachman, wrote the text. Audubon died in 1851 at the age of 65.

George Bird Grinnell, one of the founders of the National Audubon Society, chose to use Audubon's name because of his love for and keen observations of birds, his collection of magnificent paintings, and his deep concern for conservation of bird habitats. Today, the name Audubon is synonymous with birds and bird conservation all over the world.

Craft: Origami Crane

Paper folding began in Japan sometime in the sixth century. Monks brought paper into the country, probably from China, but because it was so expensive, they only used it for religious ceremonies. Slowly, folding paper became more intricate and was seen as an art form. The first book of recreational origami, *Senbazuru Orikata* (Folding of One Thousand Cranes), was published in Japan in 1797. Many origami designs depict birds and animals. One of the oldest and best-known origami figures is the crane. Here are some instructions on how to make one.

Step 1: Making a Square Base

Start with a square piece of paper, six inches by six inches or larger. Fold the paper in half diagonally. Unfold. Fold the paper in half diagonally in the other direction. Unfold. Your fold lines should create an X in the middle of your square.

Turn the paper over. Fold the paper in half to create a rectangle. Unfold. Fold the paper in half in the other direction to create a rectangle. Unfold. Your new fold lines should create a cross in the middle of your square. Notice that the X creases rise up and the cross creases sink down.

Turn your paper so it looks like a diamond, making sure that the X creases are rising up. Bring the left and right corners upward along with the top corner, letting the X creases fold up and the cross creases fold down. Open the X crease of the top corner and flatten your paper, letting the creases guide you. It should look like a smaller square with one diagonal crease mark, but have four flaps. This is called an origami square base.

Step 2: Creating a Bird Base

A bird base is a square base plus two petal folds. Turn your square base so it looks like a diamond again, with the closed point facing away from you. Take the top right flap and fold it up to the center line so that the lower open edge of the flap meets the center fold line. Repeat with the top left flap. When you are done, the folded flaps should look like an ice cream cone.

Turn your paper over and repeat, folding the right flap toward the center fold line and then the left flap toward the center fold line.

Take the closed point—the scoop of ice cream—and fold it down, creating a crease along the upper, horizontal edge of your previous two folds. Unfold it, turn the paper over, and fold down the closed point again, making a crease in the same place in the other direction. Unfold the closed point and all the flaps. You should be back to the smaller square base, but with added crease lines.

Step 3: Creating Petal Folds

Turn the paper so it looks like a diamond with the closed point facing away from you. ★Take the top layer on the open end and lift it away from you, folding it along the horizontal crease. Take the outer point of the right top flap and the outer point of the left top flap and flatten them toward the center fold. Using the already-created crease lines, bending them in the opposite direction when necessary, flatten the paper. You should now have a long diamond shape.

Turn the paper over, keeping the closed point facing away from you. Repeat the previous folds for this side now, beginning at the ★ above.

Place your paper so that the three layers of triangles—two long ones and a short one in between—are pointing away from you, and the split triangles are pointing toward you. There are two flaps on each side. Take the upper-layer right flap and fold it to the center so that the lower outer edge of the flap, the one along the split triangles, meets the center fold (same as the "ice cream cone" in step 2). Repeat with the upper-layer left flap.

Turn your paper over and repeat, folding the right flap toward the center fold and then the left flap toward the center fold. It should look like an ice cream cone again only stretched really long.

Take the upper-layer right flap and turn it to the left, like turning a page in a book. Now there should be three flaps on the left and one on the right. Turn your paper over. Take the upper-layer right flap and turn it to the left. Flatten. There should be a split in the upper section of your paper.

Step 4: Creating the Crane's Body

Take the top layer of the bottom section and push it upward toward the split points, folding it at the horizontal crease. Turn the paper over. Take the bottom section and push it toward the split points, folding it at the horizontal crease. You should have all four points pointing in the same direction, facing away from you, with two flaps on either side and a tightly creased base.

Take the upper-layer right flap and turn it to the left, like turning a page in a book. There should be three flaps on the left and one on the right.

Turn your paper over. Take what is now the upper-layer right flap and turn it to the left, like turning a page in a book. There should now be two flaps on each side with four points pointing straight up.

Step 5: Creating the Crane's Head and Tail

Hold the base of your paper in your left hand. Take the right point of the middle layer and pull it outward to a 45-degree angle. Crease the bottom, near the base. Take the tip of this right point and fold it down an inch. This is the head of your crane.

Hold the base of your paper in your right hand. Take the left point of the middle layer and pull it outward to a 45-degree angle. This is your crane's tail. Crease the bottom, near the base. Your paper should look like a three-pointed crown.

Step 6: Creating the Crane's Wings

Take the upper-layer wide center point and pull it toward you as far as it will go. Fold it down. Turn the paper over. Take the other wide center point and pull it toward you as far as it will go. Fold it down. Your crane now has wings! Lift the wings back up. Congratulations! You made your first origami crane.

Tips:

1. The bigger your sheet of paper, the easier the crane is to make. But, you can challenge yourself by using smaller and smaller squares.

2. Use light, solid-colored paper when learning this craft. Paper that is a dark color or has a pattern can make it hard to see the creases.

3. After you've made a couple of cranes, experiment using colored paper, patterned paper, and textured paper.

4. If you can't understand these printed instructions, there are several great videos on YouTube that can help you.

Fishes

Worldwide there are over thirty thousand fish species, but only a few hundred of them are caught for human consumption. From the tiniest phytoplankton to the enormous whale shark, each organism plays a role in the food web. As the world's water becomes more polluted, the temperature changes, and the number of fish shrink, you will need an in-depth understanding of conservation methods and the necessary balance within each ecosystem.

The plural of fish is usually fish. However, when referring to multiple species of fish, you say fishes. For example, if you went swimming in a lake and said that you saw lots of fish, that means that you saw lots of individual fish, maybe all of the same species. If you said that you saw lots of fishes, that means that you saw many different species.

Fisheries

A fishery is a place where fishes are raised and released, or raised and harvested for food. Fisheries can be areas where wild fish live, or they can be human-made fish farms. Fish farming is also called aquaculture or aquafarming. Around the world, over 500 million people depend on wild fisheries and aquaculture for their jobs, and billions of people depend on fish for their daily food. There are a variety of jobs within this industry, too many to make an exhaustive list. Besides a fish biologist (see chapter 10), here are a few:

Fishery leads or assistants collect data in fisheries that is then used to manage fish populations in the wild. For a lead position, you need an associate's or bachelor's degree and some field experience. For an assistant positon, you need to be working toward a degree and have some field experience. For both positions, you are expected to collect quality data, be willing to work in the water, and love spending your days hiking long distances in the outdoors.

Fishery observers collect data while living aboard a commercial fishing vessel. Training includes classroom work and at-sea training trips until the candidate gets certification. After certification, observers are sent out to collect scientific data, monitor fishing operations, and watch for compliance with current laws. They interview crew members, photograph the catch, measure selected fishes, and keep detailed records of the fishing gear used. The data collected helps researchers understand the impact of fishing on an environment and helps them make decisions about future fishing and the management of fish populations. This position requires a bachelor's degree with a major in one of the natural sciences.

Fish hatchery technicians work where fishes are incubated and raised from eggs to adults. They maintain the hatchery buildings and equipment, maintain the fishes' environment to ensure their survival, and feed the fishes. They keep accurate notes on the fishes' development and watch for signs of disease. They work with cold or warm water fishes and may stock lakes or streams once the fishes have matured. This is an entry-level position, and most people start out as temporary workers. Experience comes on the job, but having some academic background in biology or aquaculture can help you land that first temporary job.

Fishermen

Commercial fishermen fish in the deep waters of oceans or lakes, or in the shallower waters of rivers, streams, or inlets. They catch

National Fisheries

Besides state fisheries and private fish farms, the United States Fish and Wildlife Service has a system of fisheries across the nation. Here is a list of a few of those fisheries:

- **Quilcene National Fish Hatchery** in Washington raises coho salmon for release and provides eggs and finger-lings (young fish) for Native American tribal use. It also helps monitor the annual summer chum salmon runs.

- **The Saratoga National Fish Hatchery** in Wyoming is an egg-producing station for many strains of trout. The hatchery provides 2.2 million trout eggs to the Great Lakes restoration effort and 3 million eggs to other federal, state, and tribal programs. It also raises the endangered Wyoming toad and produces tadpoles and toadlets for reintroduction into the wild.

- **The Neosho National Fish Hatchery** in Missouri opened in 1888 and is the oldest federal hatchery in the United States. It stocks Lake Taneycomo with rainbow trout and releases over fifteen thousand endangered pallid sturgeons into the Missouri River each year.

- **Genoa National Fish Hatchery** in Wisconsin is work-ing to restore endangered fish like the Higgins eye pearlymussel and the coaster brook trout to the wild. It provides over twenty-six species of fish, eggs, and mussels to organizations across the country.

- **The Northeast Fishery Center** in Pennsylvania is dedicated to research. Employees' expertise is used to help fisheries make good management decisions, help recover endangered and threatened species, and help create healthy ecosystems and habitats for the fishes of the region.

- **The Warm Springs Fish Health Center** in Georgia offers state-of-the-art water chemistry analysis and diagnosis of fish diseases, including viruses, bacteria, and parasites. It also offers fish health certifications for hatcheries and private fish farms.

their fish using a wide variety of fishing gear, including poles, nets, and traps. The creatures they catch range from large tuna to tiny shrimp. A career as a commercial fisherman begins with experience as a deckhand. From there, you can move up to boatswain—the person in charge of boat maintenance and the deck crew. From boatswain, you move up to second mate, first mate, and finally captain. Once you're a captain, you'll have enough experience to buy a boat and start a business of your own.

Here's what commercial fishermen do:

- direct the fishing operations

- find the fish

- maintain the boat and gear

- manage the crew

- measure and count fish to stay within legal limits

- prepare the catch for transport

- return unwanted fish back to the water

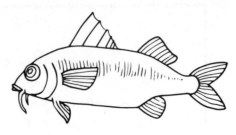

If you love to fish but don't want to be a commercial fisherman, going pro could be an option. Professional anglers start out as amateurs and work their way up the tournament ladder. Just like any sport, some people make money competing and some don't. Some colleges even have fishing teams. These colleges rank high for their fishing teams: Bethel University in Minnesota, Daytona State College in Florida, Western Illinois University, and the University of North Carolina.

TOP DOG profile

Name: Riley Wilson, DVM
Job: Wildlife Veterinarian, Commercial Fisherman, Owner of the Pet Shop
Learn about Riley Wilson's work as a zoo vet in chapter 4.

Describe your work as a commercial fisherman.

I started commercial fishing in 1973, after high school. I've owned and operated my own boat for over thirty years. My dad and I fished together for over forty years, and now I enjoy having my twin daughters join me commercial halibut fishing.

What are some of the jobs aboard a boat and that person's responsibilities?

There are many jobs when you're commercial fishing. On our halibut boat, we fish about three thousand hooks a day that need to be baited. And when we are bringing our gear in, all of the halibut needs to be cleaned and put on ice. Some days, we catch over eight thousand pounds of fish, which is a lot of cleaning! These are long days but in a very beautiful area, and I enjoy seeing all of the marine life, including whales.

What is the hardest part of commercial fishing? What is the most enjoyable part?

The hardest parts are the long days and the very physical work. My favorite part is catching all the fish, being with friends and family, and seeing all the wildlife.

What tips can you give kids who are thinking about joining a commercial fishing crew?

My advice for them would be to try to contact commercial fishing fleets. The best opportunity is to visit a commercial fishing harbor prior to the fishing season. Walk the docks and ask for any position on any boat. It's a great way of life, filled with challenges and adventure.

Protecting Animals

Every year reporters for magazines, newspapers, and television tell stories about animals whose numbers are declining in the wild. They highlight what is causing the problem and what is being done to stop it. The people who work to save animals and their habitats are called conservationists. Their work is called animal conservation.

Animal Conservation

Conservation efforts around the world focus on saving wild animals that live in threatened habitats like the Florida Everglades, the Galapagos Islands in Ecuador, or specific threatened species within a region, like the Asiatic black bears in China, the lions of Africa, or the wolves in northern Minnesota.

One way that conservationists help protect endangered species is by breeding them in captivity and then reintroducing them into the wild. When conservationists are ready to reintroduce animals into the wild, they must meet some specific criteria. There must be a thriving population in captivity, a protected habitat where the animals will be released, and enough funding to monitor their

Owls have tube-shaped eyeballs, three sets of eye-lids—one for blinking, one for sleeping, and one for cleaning—and a neck with fourteen vertebrae (twice the number of other birds), which allows them to turn their heads 270 degrees. They have feathers designed for silent flight, and they have fascinating feet. Each foot has four toes—three facing forward, one backward. But the best part is that their toes can lock in place and, when needed, one toe can swivel to face the other direction, to help the bird grasp prey or perch on a limb.

progress and educate the people in the area about the importance of the species' survival. Here are a few successful reintroductions:

- **Kihansi spray toads** from Tanzania went extinct in the wild. In 2010, they were reintroduced into the wild when one hundred toads were flown from the Bronx and Toledo Zoos to Tanzania.

- **The Guam rail** is a bird that was devastated by the introduction of snakes to the island of Guam. Conservationists captured the last twenty-nine and sent them to zoos. After twenty years in captivity, they were reintroduced into the wild, but not back to Guam. They are living on the nearby island of Rota.

- **California Condors** died off in the wild because of pesticides and lead poisoning. In 1987, the remaining twenty-two birds were captured. Within four years, researchers began releasing some back into the wild. They started rebuilding their numbers, and now there are about 200 in the wild and 200 in captivity. In October 2016, a five-and-a-half-month old female condor took flight. Condor 828 was raised entirely in the wild and is the first chick in the Pinnacles National Park to reach this momentous milestone in over 120 years!

- **Amur leopards**, "the world's rarest cat," live in Russia and China; there are only forty-five remaining in the wild and 220 in captivity. A global breeding program in zoos around the world hopes to reintroduce them back into the wild in the future.

There are many jobs related to conservation. If you are interested in protecting animals in their native habitats, here are some of the places you could work during your career.

Wild Animal Conservation Centers

Wild animal conservation centers seek to educate the public about a specific species of animal. They help reintroduce animals into their native habitats and work to preserve the animals in areas where their native habitat is shrinking. They teach the public about the importance of these animals to the ecosystem, and educate teachers, students, and government decision makers about their animals' current state in the wild and how humans are affecting them. Some centers have ambassador animals that can be observed in their native, but protected, habitat.

- International Wolf Center in Minnesota

- Grizzly and Wolf Discovery Center in West Yellowstone, Montana

- National Eagle Center in Minnesota

Conservation Gets Creative

* Around 1950, the Idaho Fish and Game Department discovered that there were too many beavers in certain areas and they were damaging rural land. Their solution: capture a bunch, load them into special cages with parachutes, and drop them from airplanes into areas where more beaver dams were needed. Fish and game employees dropped fifty-seven beavers into the Frank Church River of No Return Wilderness. No joke!

* On the Mount Ellinor trail in Washington's Olympic National Forest, mountain goats in search of salt may threaten, injure, or even kill hikers. When reports of this aggressive behavior closed the trail, US Forest Service wildlife biologist Kurt Aluzas spent the summer teaching the animals to back off. He threw rocks, shot them with a paintball gun, and yelled like a crazy man. Today, two slingshot-wielding interns remind the animals to stay away, aided by a campaign educating hikers to be aware and keep a pocket full of rocks.

* In northern California, the marbled murrelets were facing a big problem. They couldn't keep their numbers up because the Steller's jays kept finding their eggs and eating them. Local researchers devised a plan. They painted small chicken eggs to look like murrelet eggs and included a secret ingredient—carbachol. They put the eggs in easy-to-find places, and within five minutes of eating them, the jays vomited. Smart birds that they are, they soon learned to associate murrelet eggs with vomiting. Now they leave the murrelet eggs alone.

Wild Animal Rehabilitation Centers

Rehabilitation centers accept injured, orphaned, or sick animals and nurse them back to health. All animals are expected to be released into the wild. If an animal cannot be released, it is humanely euthanized or sent to an appropriate wildlife sanctuary. They often have educational exhibits and programs that inform the public about the species and their current state in the wild.

- Florida Keys Wild Bird Rehabilitation Center

- CLAWS wildlife rehabilitation and rescue organization in North Carolina

- Bear With Us Sanctuary and Rehabilitation Center in Canada

Wild and Farm Animal Sanctuaries

Sanctuaries take animals that find themselves homeless and care for them until the end of their natural lives. They do not try to adopt the animals out, nor do they sell them or let them be used for research. Animals in a sanctuary live in a protected, natural environment where their needs outweigh anyone else's. Most sanctuaries don't allow visitors. Their secondary purpose is to educate the public—through presentations at area events and school visits—about the plight of their animals and the need to treat them humanely.

- Wolves Offered Life and Friendship (WOLF) Sanctuary in Colorado

- Green Acres Farm Sanctuary in Oregon

- The Elephant Sanctuary in Tennessee

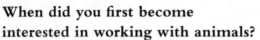

TOP DOG *profile*

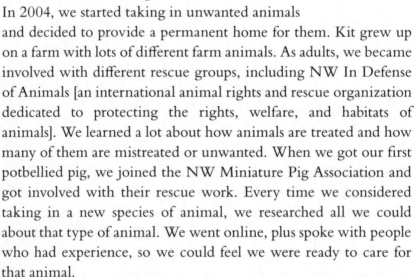

Name: Kit and John Collins
Job: Cofounders of Out to Pasture
Sanctuary

When did you first become interested in working with animals?

In 2004, we started taking in unwanted animals
and decided to provide a permanent home for them. Kit grew up
on a farm with lots of different farm animals. As adults, we became
involved with different rescue groups, including NW In Defense
of Animals [an international animal rights and rescue organization
dedicated to protecting the rights, welfare, and habitats of
animals]. We learned a lot about how animals are treated and how
many of them are mistreated or unwanted. When we got our first
potbellied pig, we joined the NW Miniature Pig Association and
got involved with their rescue work. Every time we considered
taking in a new species of animal, we researched all we could
about that type of animal. We went online, plus spoke with people
who had experience, so we could feel we were ready to care for
that animal.

How and when did you decide to start an animal sanctuary?

In 2004, Kit saw a flyer at the feed store from a local animal rescue
group asking for help. She called the number out of curiosity and
was on the phone with a rescue worker named Carmel for an hour
finding out all about what the group did. Carmel had another job
during the week and did her rescue work on weekends. She would
transport animals from bad homes to better adoptive homes. She
had no land and no money, just a desire to help unwanted animals.
This inspired us since we had more than Carmel did, yet she was
doing more than we were to help animals. We decided right then
that doing something would be better than doing nothing.

126

We started partnering with different rescue groups to take in the animals that they were unable to adopt out due to old age, bad behavior, health problems, or other issues.

Describe the steps you took to get your sanctuary going.

We created a nonprofit organization with the help of an attorney. We also had to put up fences and build shelters each time we took in more animals. Being vegans, we networked with the vegan and vegetarian community to raise money. We have found that just about everyone wants to help animals and is supportive of our mission.

We have a series of fundraisers, such as yard sales, dinners, movie nights, open houses, and other events, throughout the year to raise money.

What is life like at the sanctuary?

We care for llamas, donkeys, farm pigs, potbellied pigs, goats, sheep, rabbits, cats, dogs, and many types of poultry. We spend two hours in the morning and an hour at night cleaning stalls and duck pools, plus feeding and watering all the animals. On other days, we also have more chores such as scrubbing all the water dishes, cleaning more enclosures, and going to the feed store and the hardware store. We also give tours to visitors. If an animal is sick, we immediately call the vet and make arrangements to have that animal seen as soon as possible.

We deal with a lot of emails and phone calls [from people] asking us to help them find a new home for their animal. If we can't take the animal in, we contact other animal sanctuaries and post something online to help find a home. We have to carefully screen anyone who responds to make sure they will provide a good home.

What is the hardest part of owning a sanctuary? What is the most rewarding part?

The hardest part is not being able to take in every animal. Also, having to constantly be fundraising is a challenge. The most rewarding part is seeing a neglected animal decide that humans aren't all bad. Watching them regain their trust in humans makes us very happy.

What tips do you have for kids who are interested in pursuing a career caring for animals?
Go visit and volunteer at different sanctuaries. Once the organization gets to know you, they will think of you if there is a job opening.

What is your favorite animal and why?
Poppy, the eight hundred–pound farm pig, is my favorite. She is like an eight hundred–pound puppy! Poppy loves belly rubs and attention. In the summer, she will run over to be sprayed with the hose. If you talk to her, she will grunt back.

Sanctuaries and Rescues around the World

- **The Agra Bear Rescue Facility** in Agra, Northern India, is India's leading conservation organization. It rescues native animals and is best known for its rescue of India's endangered sloth bears.

- **Boon Lott's Sanctuary** near Sukhothai, North Thailand, rescues and rehabilitates Thai elephants.

- **Chengdu Moon Bear Rescue Center** in Chengdu, China, rescues critically endangered Asiatic black bears, also known as moon bears because of the white, moon-shaped patch on their chests.

- **Lone Pine Koala Sanctuary** in Brisbane, Australia, is the world's oldest and largest Koala rescue. They also care for kangaroos, platypuses, and birds of prey.

- **SanWild Wildlife Sanctuary** in Limpopo Province, South Africa, rescues and rehabilitates wild animals like impala, kudu, blue wildebeest, rhinos, and aardvarks.

- **Sepilok Orangutan Sanctuary** in the Malaysian Sabah District, Northern Borneo, is a rainforest sanctuary that cares for orphaned and injured animals like sun bears, gibbons, and elephants, but especially endangered orangutans.

- **The Vervet Monkey Foundation** in Tzaneen, South Africa, provides a home for injured, orphaned, or rescued monkeys.

In 2010, Jeneria Lekilelei, a young warrior from the Samburu tribe of northern Kenya, started a lion protection program called Warrior Watch with other moran (warrior-aged men) of his tribe. They use their skills as trackers and wildlife observers to ease conflict between herders and big cats by warning herders when a cat is in the area, building fences to protect livestock, intervening when a herder plans to hunt a cat who has killed one of his animals, and educating herders about the importance of big cats to the ecosystem and economy. Jeneria says, "Warriors are the eyes and ears in the bush and involving them is key to the conservation and security of [my] region's wildlife and people."[1]

Jobs in Conservation

Game wardens are sometimes called conservation officers or wildlife officers. They work for the federal or state government as the law enforcement officers who monitor and manage wildlife populations. They patrol on foot, on horseback, on four-wheelers, and by plane. They track and arrest poachers, watch for overfishing or overhunting, and investigate hunting accidents. Another responsibility is educating the public on the need for conservation in their area, and about the laws that govern use of the land and hunting and fishing in the area. Specific education and experience requirements for this job vary by state, and the US Fish and Wildlife Service has its own detailed job requirements and training procedures.

Working as a game warden can be dangerous. They are allowed to carry guns because they go into remote areas where backup could be miles away. It is common for them to find drug manufacturing labs and illegal marijuana farms or to find people violating hunting or fishing laws. Arresting suspects in any of these situations can be risky. Game wardens also face dangerous wild animals and have to work outside in all kinds of weather conditions.

Wildlife rehabilitators work under the guidance of a wildlife veterinarian. They help rescue orphaned or injured animals, assess an animal's illness or injury, administer first aid and physical therapy, and help raise babies and release them into the wild. Rehabilitators need extensive knowledge about many species, including their native habitat history, their nutritional needs, their unique behavior issues, and the best ways to keep them confined. This can be a dangerous job, and understanding each animal's "fight or flight" reaction is important. The skills needed to work as an animal rehabilitator can be developed through hands-on experience or course work in wildlife biology, zoology, or similar veterinary medicine courses.

It is illegal in every state to try to rehabilitate a wild animal without a permit. Federal laws protect wild birds, and state laws protect most other wild mammals and reptiles. Before getting a permit, you must meet the requirements of your state, which may include specialized training, internship experience, and a written or oral exam. To rehabilitate migratory birds, you must get a permit from the US Fish and Wildlife Service.

 # SPOTLIGHT

Harriet Lawrence Hemenway (1858–1960), The Mother of Conservation and Founder of the First Audubon Society

Harriet Lawrence was born in 1858. Her father was very wealthy, an abolitionist, and a strong supporter of education. When it came time for Harriet to marry, he approved of a young man named Augustus Hemenway, a graduate of Harvard University and a man whose family could tout deep New England roots. Harriet was comfortable in a society where her name was synonymous with great wealth and political power.

In 1896, Hemenway read an article about the plume (feather) trade. It described how millions of birds were being killed for their feathers, just so ladies could have beautiful, ornate hats to wear. It talked about the total destruction of nesting areas and how newly hatched chicks were being left to starve to death or be eaten by predators. She learned that feathers were selling at about twenty dollars an ounce, higher than the price of gold!

She was so outraged by the story that she decided to do something. She enlisted the help of her cousin, Minna B. Hall, and together they organized tea parties to persuade their friends to stop wearing feathered hats. Hemenway once said, "We sent out circulars asking the women to join a society for the protection of birds, especially the egret. Some women joined and some who preferred to wear feathers would not join."[3] By the end of their campaign, the cousins had about nine hundred women pledged to join their cause.

At the time, women held little political power. It would take another twenty-four years for them to get the right to vote. So Hemenway decided to persuade her husband and as many businessmen and scientists as she could find to help. With their support, she founded the Massachusetts Audubon Society, the first and oldest of many that would later make up the National Audubon Society.

In 1897, Hemenway and the newly formed Audubon Society forced the Massachusetts legislature to write a bill outlawing the wild bird feather trade. Unfortunately, the rest of the country didn't follow Massachusetts's lead. It took several years for other states to pass laws of their own, protecting birds in their regions.

Because of Hemenway's dedication to birds, the plume trade was eventually stopped. She worked to pass the first federal conservation law, the 1900 Lacey Act, which prohibited the interstate transport of any wild species killed in violation of state laws. In 1913, the Weeks–McLean Act, also known as the Migratory Bird Act, was passed, prohibiting the hunting of birds for their feathers.

In 1920, the United States Supreme Court upheld the Migratory Bird Treaty Act of 1918. As a result of that decision, Justice Oliver Wendell Holmes wrote that protecting birds was in our nation's interest and, "But for the treaty and the statute, there soon might be no birds for any powers to deal with."

Hemenway's dedication to the preservation of birds didn't end with enacting laws. Throughout her lifetime, she worked with the Audubon Society to purchase native bird habitat and set it aside for future generations. She was also a strong advocate for teaching children the need to protect vulnerable species. She died in 1960 at the age of 103.

Quiz: A Lot Like Us

What separates humans from the rest of the animals on earth? The answer might be more difficult to define than you think. Some species, like parrots, are able to develop cultures of their own, dolphins and elephants possess self-awareness, and dogs' brains process voices and emotions in a similar way to humans.

From the lists below, match the animals to the human-like traits they can exhibit.

1. I help other females in my troop to give birth, much like a human midwife.

2. I laugh when I am tickled.

3. I like to keep things clean, and I put away my toys when I'm done playing with them.

4. I have a long memory. I remember my human and animal friends and lovingly greet them. I remember my enemies and react with anger or disdain when I see them. After a traumatic incident, I can suffer from post–traumatic stress disorder, just like humans do.

5. With training, I can use a toilet and even flush it after I'm done.

6. I grimace when I'm in pain.

7. I get upset and stressed when my baby feels pain. I grieve if one of my children dies.

8. I communicate using a variety of hand gestures. I can learn human sign language from my trainers and tell them about my past experiences.

9. I call my friends by name, and sometimes I talk in my sleep.

10. Like a human gambler, I will choose a high-risk gamble for a great reward, rather than settle for a guaranteed smaller reward.

Animals

a. Cat
b. Chicken
c. Dolphin
d. Elephant
e. Gorilla

f. Monkey
g. Mouse
h. Pig
i. Pigeon
j. Rat

Answer Key: 1:f 2:j 3:h 4:d 5:a 6:g 7:b 8:e 9:c 10:i

Animal Rescue

There are many people across the nation who work diligently to protect domestic animals from abuse and neglect. They work for breed-specific animal rescues, animal rehabilitation centers, animal shelters, and sanctuaries. There are hundreds, if not thousands, of jobs available within each of these categories, ranging from veterinarians to basic animal care staff. Here's a general description of each category.

Societies

The terms "humane society" and "society for the prevention of cruelty to animals" are descriptive phrases. Much like the word "bank" in Wells Fargo Bank or Bank of America, it tells you something about the organization, but it does not mean that the organizations are connected. Banks are independent of each other, and so are humane societies.

Societies work with federal, state, and local governments to pass laws that protect animals. They also strive to raise awareness of the plight of abused and neglected animals, the dramatic loss of native habitats, and the need to protect endangered animals from extinction. Some societies have shelters that care for animals until they can be adopted.

- 🐾 The American Society for the Prevention of Cruelty to Animals (ASPCA)

- 🐾 People for the Ethical Treatment of Animals (PETA)

- 🐾 The American Humane Society

Domestic Animal Rescues

Domestic animal rescues use a foster care system and usually don't have facilities of their own. Animals are located and then sent to a foster home, where they stay until they find a "fur-ever" home. Rescue animals come from unsafe homes, shelters that euthanize, owners who don't want them anymore, or families after an owner has died.

Rescues are often breed specific and take their work very seriously. They require an application, home visit, references, a veterinarian recommendation, education about the breed's characteristics, and an adoption fee that helps cover the ongoing expenses and transportation of animals. Don't plan on getting a breeding animal from a rescue. Rescues require that all animals be spayed or neutered before adoption. Some rescues will transport a dog up to a thousand miles if they find it a good home!

🐾 Midwest Shiba Inu Rescue

🐾 Rural Animal Rescue and Foster Society in Tennessee

🐾 National Anatolian Shephard Dog Rescue Network

The most dangerous animal in the world is the mosquito. Each year, mosquitos kill over 750,000 people! How? By transmitting dangerous diseases like dengue fever, yellow fever, Zika virus, West Nile virus, and—the greatest killer of them all—malaria, which killed over four hundred thousand people in 2015.[4] Scientists have made a breakthrough in genetic research. By changing the genes in a mosquito's DNA, they can make its offspring unable to reproduce and thus drive them into extinction. It is a great scientific breakthrough and could save millions of lives. However, in a world where species are going extinct at a rate unseen since the time of the dinosaurs, should scientists deliberately cause another one to disappear? And, after the mosquito, then what? Should they also get rid of those nasty lice or those pesky mice? Who decides if a species lives or dies? As genetic research advances, this is only the first of many serious questions that you, the next generation of animal researchers, must answer.

Domestic Animal Shelters

Domestic animal shelters find their animals in the same ways as rescues. The difference is that they house them on-site and adopt them out to almost anyone who wants them. You will need to fill out an application and pay a fee, but otherwise, you won't face much scrutiny over your ability to care for the animal. Shelters require that the animal be spayed or neutered, and many implant an identification microchip. In the past, most shelters euthanized animals that were not adopted within a certain time frame. Today, some are becoming no-kill shelters and keeping the animal until it is adopted.

- Austin Pets Alive! in Texas

- Best Friends Animal Society in Utah

- Richmond Society for the Prevention of Cruelty to Animals in Virginia

Domestic Animal Retirement Centers

Ever wonder what happens to pets when their owners can no longer care for them or die, and there's no one willing to give them a new home? Now there's an answer—pet retirement centers. This growing trend offers pet owners peace of mind that their beloved animals will be cared for when they can no longer do the job themselves.

Retirement centers usually take only one type of pet, but some are open to cats, dogs, birds, and other more exotic animals. Someone is on duty 24 hours a day to make sure all the animals are fed, groomed, and played with, and that their medical needs are met.

Animal retirement centers can be nonprofit or for-profit businesses, and they care for animals until they die. An animal's care is paid for by concerned citizens or by the owner, who pays an enrollment fee to guarantee their pets' placement and then sets up an endowment or a trust to cover future costs. Some centers are connected to university veterinary programs. All retirement centers may euthanize but only as part of end-of-life care.

- 🐾 Paradigm Farms equine retirement in Tennessee

- 🐾 The Shannon Foundation for farm animals and dogs in Missouri

- 🐾 House with a Heart Senior Pet Sanctuary, a nonprofit in Maryland

||||||||||||||||||||||||||||||||||||||||||||||||||||||||||||||||||||||||||||||||||||||||||||||||||||||||||||

Name: Carter and Olivia Ries
Age: 15 and 13
Job (when not studying!): Cofounders of One More Generation (OMG)

When did you first discover your love for endangered animals and decide that they needed your help?
Olivia: Well, it all started back in 2009 when my aunt was in South Africa and she brought back two certificates that said that we were the proud parents of cheetahs! The next year, when it was time to renew our adoptions, I asked my dad, why do animals need to be adopted?

Carter: He told her that if there weren't any agencies like the one we were adopting our cheetahs from, then there might not be cheetahs around for our kids to see.

Olivia: That made me upset and I started to cry. I told my dad that I want to save cheetahs for my kids to someday see. He tried to calm me down by saying that when I got older, I could start my own company to help save animals. Well I took that as, "Dad said we could start our own company."

138

Carter: We knew that if we didn't do something right now, then nobody would, and the animals might be gone forever.

What was your first project to help save endangered animals?

Carter: From the beginning we raised money and awareness for the cheetahs we had just adopted. On a local level, our first endangered species we helped were the rattlesnakes. We had heard about the rattlesnake roundups and what people were doing to the snakes. We knew we had to step in. We convinced a county to stop killing the rattlesnakes and turn their event into a wildlife festival where they showed the good in snakes and [did] not kill them.

Olivia: On an international level, our first effort was to try and save rhinos from being poached to the brink of extinction. We collected ten thousand letters from people around the world to raise awareness about rhino poaching. We traveled back to South Africa to deliver these letters to the minister of environmental affairs.

When and why did you decide to start your nonprofit organization, One More Generation?

Carter: Once we realized that animals needed our help, we sprang into action. That was back in 2009 when we were seven and eight years old. One More Generation is "a nonprofit organization dedicated to the preservation of endangered species, our communities, and our environment. Our goal is to ensure the well-being of our planet for at least One More Generation . . . and beyond."

Olivia: As we learned about other companies who are working to save animals, we realized that we could do the same, so we bugged our dad until he finally heard us and helped us start OMG.

Describe your current endangered species campaigns.

Carter: We recently launched our orangutan letter-writing campaign in an effort to raise awareness about what is happening to orangutans and why they are losing their natural habitat. Indonesia is where the orangutans live, and their rainforest is being cut down because of the palm oil industries, logging industries, and the mining industries who are completely destroying their homeland just for resources. We are asking everyone to write letters to the president of Indonesia, asking him to get serious about saving the species before it is too late. We have been invited to speak at a conference in Jakarta, where we will be hand delivering all the letters we collect from around the world to the president of Indonesia.

The Mountain Gorilla

As the world wrestles with population growth and global warming, it is important to consider the plight of the animal that is genetically closest us, the giant gorilla, with whom we share about 98 percent of our DNA. The gorilla, along with the chimpanzee, orangutan, and bonobo are the last four species of great apes alive on Earth. And they are in danger of going extinct.

There are fewer than 1,000 mountain gorillas living in the wild. Their home is in central Africa in an area where increases in human population means that their forest habitat is being destroyed to make room for food production. Because we are so genetically similar, the gorillas also face danger from human diseases like flu, pneumonia, and Ebola. A third reason for their predicament is unrest in the three countries that surround their territory: the Democratic Republic of Congo, Rwanda, and Uganda. The main way that conservationists try to fund their efforts to protect the mountain gorilla is through tourism. Unfortunately, tourism depends on peace in the region, something that is elusive in this part of the world.

Olivia: We are working on several projects. We are still working to raise awareness about what is happening to the rhinos, and the orangutan letter-writing campaign because we learned that they are losing their habitat at an alarming rate! We also learned about plastic pollution while we were helping with the animal rescue efforts during the BP [formerly British Petroleum and one of the world's seven humungous oil and gas companies] oil spill in the Gulf [of Mexico], and we have since created an award-winning plastic and recycling awareness curriculum that teaches students about the issue and, more importantly, how they can be part of the solution. Did you know that each year over one hundred thousand marine mammals and over one million seabirds die from ingesting plastic?

Describe your conservation seminars.
Carter: We speak at many different places, and we enjoy doing it. We teach many different people, but we always target the youth because they don't yet have issues adults deal with so they understand. They love animals, and they will listen to another youth better than they will listen to an adult. Our goal is to empower the youth to stand up and make a difference, to seek out their passion and fulfill that. It doesn't matter if they care about animals, the ocean, or even helping the homeless; you just have to follow that passion.

Olivia: We speak all over the place, from churches to UN [United Nations] meetings. Our audience can be all kinds of people. Our goal is to inspire one person in the audience (the more the merrier), and if we inspire that person, they will go and tell their friends, and their friends will tell others, and so on. We have been to South Africa twice. We recently were invited to speak in Vietnam. We are going to Costa Rica; Honolulu; New Delhi; and Jakarta, Indonesia, later this year—all in an effort to reach as many people as we can and share our passion with others. We have spoken to audiences as small as three people to crowds of over three thousand, and we love it.

Describe your favorite experience with an animal.

Carter: My favorite experience has got to be in South Africa when I was at a rhino orphanage. I heard the horror stories behind why they were here, but then got to see their happy side. I enjoyed spending time with them, feeding them, and sitting beside them as they fell asleep. It was a truly amazing experience and I wish to do it over again someday.

Olivia: That's hard to say because I work with animals a lot, but probably my favorite is when we got to play with and feed cheetahs at the cheetah rescue center in South Africa. I also loved comforting the baby black rhino that had its leg broken by poachers because she was trying to stop them from killing her mother. Sadly, the baby had to be put to sleep two weeks after we were there because they could not fix her leg. I also loved working with the sea turtles at the Marine Mammal and Sea Turtle Rescue center in the Gulf during the BP oil spill. They are so cute. ;-)

What books, magazines, or organizations do you enjoy?

Carter: I like adventure books and always have. Myths and series books have always intrigued me by how they keep you on the edge until the next book comes out or the next time you can go to the library to find that book. I always loved that. The organizations I like are the ones that care about animals and the environment. Yes, there are some out there that are in it for the money, but the places that truly care about the planet as much as my family does, those are the organizations I enjoy watching make a difference.

Olivia: I love Nat Geo; I actually write for Nat Geo every Wednesday. Right now, I am learning sign language, so I have a book that I am reading for that. And for the organization, I like a place called AWARE [Atlanta Wild Animal Rescue Effort]. They take in injured animals and rehab them back into the wild. I also volunteer on Sundays at AWARE.

World's Largest Gorilla

Fossils found in China uncovered a species of giant gorilla that stood almost ten feet tall and weighed from 500 to 1000 pounds (270–500 kilograms). *Gigantopithecus* lived in the tropical forests of southeast Asia for millions of years, and went extinct about 100,000 years ago. Scientists think that their great size, and their dependency on a diet of fruit, meant that they could not adapt when the climate cooled and the forests turned into grassland.

Where do you see yourself in ten years?

Carter: One More Generation has come a long way since it started, and I can definitely see myself doing this work in the future. In the next ten years, I see myself worrying less about the problems I see now with this world. I see myself teaching more youth about matters that truly mean something. Teaching them about the oceans and plastic pollution and how they can be the solution. Showing the world that we all need to step in because if we all keep waiting, then we will be right back at the start. I want my children to see the same animals I got to see. To boil it down, I see myself teaching the next generation of leaders how to be the solution.

Olivia: Well, in ten years I will be twenty-three years old. I will most likely still be running OMG, and I hope to go to college to learn how to be a vet.

Training Animals and Animals in Entertainment

Animals are infinitely fascinating, and we find them extremely entertaining. Go online to YouTube and look at the millions of cat videos, and you will begin to understand our intense passion for them. We love dogs that perform tricks, horses that run fast, and dolphins that flip out of the water. Whenever there's an animal around, people take notice. So how do they get those animals to do what they do? It takes training. If you are interested in training animals, read on to learn about some of the areas where you can build a career.

Quiz: History's Coolest Animal Actors

Since the beginning of television, many shows have featured animals as part of the cast. Below is a list of famous animals from television's past. Can you match the names of the characters to the shows in which they appeared?

Female African buffalo vote on which direction the herd should move. They stand up, face the direction they want to go, and then lie back down. Majority wins. If the vote is split, the herd splits and grazes in different areas for a while. Pigeons give every bird a vote on where the flock goes, but their social structure ensures that some birds always lead while others follow. And, honey bees use their queen for egg laying, not for decision-making. Worker and drone bees make the decisions. Scout bees perform a waggle dance to communicate where they think the hive should go. When there is more than one opinion, it becomes a popularity contest to try to sway the colony's decision. Scout bees that keep dancing after their site is rejected get butted in the head.

1. This chimpanzee crossed the United States with BJ, his truck-driving friend, in a 1979 sitcom.

2. This talking black cat gave guidance and caused mischief for Sabrina in the 1990s sitcom *Sabrina the Teenage Witch*.

3. Despite his gentle name, this lion frightened the family's guests in the 1960s series *The Addams Family*.

4. This animal was the focus of a 1960s show about a game warden in the Everglades and his family's pet black bear.

5. When the Lone Ranger shouted, "Hi-yo, _____, away!" in his films, television, and radio shows dating back to 1938, this trusty steed carried him wherever he needed to go in the pursuit of justice.

6. A dog played this character in the 1990s sitcom *Full House*, and went on to star in Air Bud, a movie about a dog who plays basketball.

7. This pig played checkers, delivered newspapers, and won painting contests in the 1960s show *Green Acres*.

8. This horse in a 1960s sitcom could talk—but usually kept that a secret from everyone but his owner.

9. This bottlenose dolphin helped his owner enforce regulations on the marine preserve where they lived in the 1964 series that shares his name.

10. This original star of the movie screen later became a television star from 1954 to 1973, and is the main character in many popular books.

Famous Critters

a. Lassie

b. Gentle Ben

c. Salem

d. Bear

e. Silver

f. Flipper

g. Arnold

h. Comet

i. Mr. Ed

j. Kitty Kat

Answers: 1:d 2:c 3:j 4:b 5:e 6:h 7:g 8:i 9:f 10:a

Animal Trainers

From a loud call that brings a herd of cows into the barn to hand signals that direct a dog into a collapsed building, humans have trained animals in a myriad of ways to make their and our lives easier, safer, more comfortable, and more exciting. Everything that's done with an animal takes training. Pets are often trained by their owners, but working animals, zoo animals, and those used for entertainment are trained by skilled animal trainers.

Animal trainers work with animals for the following reasons:

- for their individual care—to tolerate physical exams, grooming, clipping nails, cleaning teeth, and stepping on or off a scale

- for ease of transport—to easily enter crates, trailers, or barns, or to move from pen to pen

- for obedience—to aid their socialization, promote non-aggressive behavior, and perform in competitions or for entertainment

- for law enforcement—for sniffing out drugs, gun powder, and cadavers; patrolling neighborhoods and apprehending bad guys; tracking criminals or missing people; and guarding facilities

- for service to disabled people—to monitor for seizures, help with daily chores, and help prevent anxiety attacks

- for social therapy in hospitals, schools, and senior centers

Teaching an animal to follow instructions requires a great deal of patience and an understanding of how animals think. To train most animals, you'll need a combination of academic classes and hands-on experience. These skills can come from volunteer opportunities, apprenticeships, internships, or an associate of science degree in animal care and management. However, if you want to train marine mammals or zoo animals, you will need a bachelor's degree in biology, zoology, or a related science.

Your first step to becoming an animal trainer is to decide what animal you want to train. The most common is dogs, but horses, birds, and marine mammals are also popular. Your choice will determine what training you need to pursue.

In an associate's degree program, you will learn about:

- 🐾 animal behavior management

- 🐾 animal care and handling

- 🐾 animal nutrition

- 🐾 capture and restraint

- 🐾 conservation

- 🐾 euthanasia

- 🐾 animal welfare laws

- 🐾 record keeping

- 🐾 wildlife education

We love our athletes and our sports teams—including those featuring animal companions. From the Alaskan Iditarod to the Triple Crown races, animals have entertained us in competitions that demonstrate their strength, agility, and spirit. Horse racing is one competition that everyone recognizes, followed by dog racing and bull fighting. But there are other races happening around the world that you may not have heard about. Here are a few of them:

- 🐾 In the town of Talbot, Australia, they race yabbie, a freshwater crustacean found in dams in many places around the country. Each race is short and very slow.

- In Russia they have the Pig Olympics. Pigs compete in swimming, running, and even soccer games, trying to win a gold medal.

- Pigeon racing is a sport in many nations around the world. The birds are released and then timed to see which one returns home the fastest. Sometimes a bird wins by only a few seconds.

- One of the cutest competitions is rabbit racing. The sport is popular in Scandinavia, which has over fifty rabbit-jumping clubs, and in the United Kingdom. The rabbits compete in a timed race that includes multiple obstacles for them to jump over. The first American Hopping Association race was held in 2011.

- In Nepal, India, and Thailand, elephant polo is a popular sport. Two people ride on each animal; one steers while the other tries to hit a ball into the goal.

- The World Snail Racing Championships are held in the United Kingdom each year, but smaller competitions are held around the world. This slow but steady race takes place on a small circular track, and each tiny participant has a number painted on its shell.

- In the United States and the United Kingdom, hamster racing is popular. Hamsters in tiny vehicles compete in a thirty-foot (nine-meter) race.

Where Animal Trainers Work

- animal rescues

- aquariums

- 🐾 circuses

- 🐾 for movie or television productions

- 🐾 for owners of competition animals

- 🐾 for owners of family pets

- 🐾 ranches

- 🐾 sanctuaries

- 🐾 zoos

Punxsutawney Phil is a groundhog that lives in Punxsutawney, Pennsylvania, and has the big job of predicting the arrival of spring every year on Groundhog Day. On February 2, Phil comes out of his hole and either sees his shadow and returns to his nest, which means six more weeks of winter, or doesn't see his shadow and stays aboveground, which means spring has arrived. In 1986, Phil met President Ronald Reagan, and in 1995, he appeared on the *Oprah Winfrey Show*. When Phil is not predicting the end of winter, he is cared for by a group known as the Inner Circle.

Name: Hope Luttrell
Age: 16
Job (when not studying!): Rodeo Rider

YOUNG PUP profile

When did you first discover your love for horses and start competing in rodeos?

I started competing when I was two years old. When I was just beginning, I competed in the peewee rodeos. Realizing that I had a love for this sport, I later advanced to the junior high rodeo and currently compete in high school rodeo and amateur rodeos such as the NPRA (Northwest Professional Rodeo Association). Since the sixth grade, I have qualified every year for nationals, and when I was in junior high, I won Rookie of the Year in Oregon, meaning I did better than anyone else their first year competing at the junior high level.

As soon as I was done with my junior high career, I advanced to high school rodeo, where the competitors are older, faster, and tougher.

Describe some of the struggles you've faced during your rodeo career.

As a freshman, I knew barely any people and only had a few friends, so I had a hard time competing at first. I had to borrow horses because I couldn't find one that fit me. About halfway through the season, I found an amazing rope horse that I still have. When I first got her, she was only a breakaway horse. I didn't have a goat-tying horse, and I was jumping on other peoples' horses that I had not ridden before. Finally, I decided to teach her how to help me goat tie. By the end of the season, we qualified for state finals in that event. I also qualified for the National High School Rodeo Finals in goat tying and light rifle shooting, making me one of four freshmen to qualify out of several hundred. I got the opportunity to travel to Rock Springs, Wyoming. I ended up thirty-second in the nation out of hundreds of other goat tyers worldwide.

From then on, I competed in the NPRA and traveled all of Oregon and Washington competing in breakaway roping and barrel racing. Six weeks before the 2015 finals, I was running barrels in Tygh Valley, Oregon, and my horse stumbled and fell on me, breaking my collarbone so badly that I had to have surgery.

I now have a plate and five screws in my shoulder. Missing the last six rodeos, I got bumped out of the top twelve in breakaway, but I continued to hold my spot in barrel racing. Even though I was still in physical therapy, I competed. I borrowed a horse because my horse, Mojo, was still injured from the accident. And I won the barrel racing Rookie of the Year!

What do you enjoy most about competition?
What I love most about traveling the nation to compete is meeting new people and competing in front of the large crowds. I live for the crowd screaming and shouting as I make my run or rope. And when I put together a good run, I love when they go crazy. I love the long drives, the late nights, and being with good friends. There isn't much to dislike.

What has the rodeo experience taught you?
I have learned how to take care of myself and my horses under most circumstances. I have learned how to train horses, help kids, and interact with people, but it has also showed me how important my family and horses are to my life.

Training horses is really an incredible thing. They are so intelligent and learn quickly. When [I] get a good horse, they teach me just as much as I teach them. To train a horse to their best ability, it takes lots of time and patience. It is an everyday activity. Every morning I wake up and go outside and feed all the horses. I then head to school. As soon as I get home, I ride my horses and practice, and then do the nightly feeding.

Where do you see yourself in ten years?
I see myself graduating from college with my bachelor's degree in animal science and attending pro rodeos, doing breakaway and barrel racing. I plan on continuing to rodeo when I get to the college level and, when I'm old enough, continuing to compete at the professional level.

||||||||||||||||||||||||||||||||||||||||||||||||||||||||||||||||||||||||||||||||||||||||||||||||||||||||||||||

Other Jobs for Animal Trainers

Alligator wranglers use whatever means they can to remove alligators and crocodiles from places where they aren't welcome. It is a dangerous and low-paying job. If you're still interested, you can take classes at the Colorado Gators Reptile Park and learn how to safely handle these strong animals. Graduates of their classes earn a Certificate of Insanity!

Falconers train birds of prey. These birds are used for hunting, competition, entertainment, and pest control. If you want to train as a falconer, plan to work outside all the time. These birds need training year-round in all weather conditions. There are three levels of training: apprentice, general (two years), and master (seven years). To start as an apprentice, you need a permit from your state's Fish and Wildlife Service, a sponsor who is at the general or master level, a mews to properly house your bird, and special equipment like gloves, leashes, and perches.

Horse trainers are also called equine trainers. They help horses learn to accept a rider, race other horses, and perform in shows and rodeos. They also help horses overcome anxiety or behavior issues due to abuse or trauma. To become a horse trainer, you'll start as an apprentice, stable hand, or horse groomer and work your way up. There are some colleges that offer courses in equine studies.

There are other jobs working with horses:

- barn manager

- breeder

- circus performer

- competition judge

- dude-ranch hand

- farrier

- horse camp counselor

- riding instructor or guide

- rodeo clown

- rodeo rider

Insect wranglers handle the insects that appear on television shows or in movies: flies, maggots, cockroaches, spiders, or any other bug that the script calls for. They raise their own bugs or buy them from suppliers. Wranglers are responsible for making the bugs act in the way the director envisions. Insects can't be trained, so the wrangler researches each bug to learn what motivates them. They use lines of sugar to direct ants and lemon Pledge to keep spiders away from specific areas, or they blow air through a straw to move spiders in different directions. The more insects you understand, the more work you can get.

Jockeys ride racehorses. To be a jockey, you should be between five foot two and five foot four inches tall and weigh about 110 pounds. You must be a careful but fearless rider. Jockeys need to be patient and calm, and they must have the ability to get a horse to relax and set a good running pace. There are two jockey training schools in the United States: the North American Racing Academy in Kentucky and the Frank Garza Jockey School in California. You can also learn by working on a horse farm, but be prepared to start out cleaning stalls and mending fences. If you're lucky, you will get to exercise the horses. Then, if you show promise, someone will train you to ride in races. A career as a jockey is unstable and dangerous. Pursue it only if you can't imagine doing anything else.

Lion tamers train wild cats, including leopards, panthers, tigers, and cheetahs. They work for zoos, wildlife sanctuaries, theme parks, and circuses. Their two goals are to entertain the public and to keep themselves, the animals, and the public safe. Their education is the same as any animal trainer, but focused on the big cats.

 # SPOTLIGHT

Julie Krone (1963–) First Female Jockey to Win the Belmont Stakes and the Breeders' Cup

Julieann Krone was born on July 24, 1963, and grew up on a farm in Eau Claire, Michigan. Her mother, a prizewinning show rider, had Julie riding horses by the time she was two. With a fire in her belly and riding in her blood, Krone was winning competitions by the age of five.

When she was fourteen, she saw eighteen-year-old Steve Cauthen win the 1978 Triple Crown. From that moment, she knew she was going to be a jockey. Besides the drive, she also had the body for the sport, four foot ten inches tall and slightly built.

Teased in school for her tiny size and high-pitched voice, Krone found comfort in poetry and horses. When she was fifteen, her mother forged a birth certificate so Krone could claim that she was old enough to work at Churchill Downs. Her first job was as a "hot walker," walking the thoroughbred horses to cool them off after a workout or race. She loved the job so much that she quit high school during her senior year and quickly advanced to exercise rider and then apprentice jockey. On February 17, 1981, at the age of seventeen, she won her first professional race.

As a woman in a male-dominated career, Krone faced sexism, threats of violence, and hostile moves from male riders during competitions. Over time, Krone gave as good as she got, and eventually she earned their respect. But it was her patience while working with the highly strung thoroughbreds that got her the most admiration. She seemed to effortlessly guide a horse around the track, keeping him relaxed until it was time to push forward and take the lead.

In 1991, she rode in her first Kentucky Derby at Churchill Downs, and she became the first woman to ride in the Belmont Stakes. The Kentucky Derby, the Belmont Stakes, and the Preakness are the three races that make up the Triple Crown competition. She didn't win either race.

Two years later, she got a second chance to compete in the Belmont Stakes riding a horse named Colonial Affair that everyone thought was a long shot to win. With skill and tactical shrewdness, she guided the animal around the track and into the history books, becoming the first woman to win a Triple Crown race. Krone's popularity exploded. She became known as the best jockey of her time and a jewel in the eyes of racing fans.

After the Belmont win, Krone faced a different challenge. She was riding a horse named Seattle Way down the homestretch when suddenly another horse cut in front of them. Seattle Way's foreleg hit the hind leg of the other horse, sending both him and Krone tumbling to the ground. The crash was devastating. Krone's ankle was crushed, her elbow was broken, and a passing horse kicked her in the chest. Krone was rushed to the hospital and underwent two operations to repair the damage.

It took Krone's body eight months to recover, but it was healing her mind that took true courage. For the first time in her life, she felt fear and had to cope with the idea of the very real danger that was a part of her sport. She struggled with nightmares, insomnia, depression, and pain. She fought long and hard against the idea of never riding again.

She returned to competition in 1994, but in early 1995 fell off her horse again, this time breaking both of her hands. Krone rode for another four years, continuing to win races. When she retired in 1999, she had tallied over 3,500 wins. In 2000, she was inducted into the National Museum of Racing's Hall of Fame. She returned to thoroughbred racing in 2002, and the next year she became the first female jockey to win the Breeders' Cup. She retired permanently from competitive racing in 2004.

Today, Krone works as a spokesperson for post traumatic stress disorder (PTSD), an illness that affects many Americans. She is a role model for young girls, teaching them that what matters most is not the races you win or the money you earn, but knowing that when you fall down, you can get back up and ride on!

Animal/Wildlife Photographers

Earning a living as a wildlife photographer is hard. The field is competitive, and the pathway to success is as varied as the people pursuing it. Some photographers are self-taught, some get a bachelor's degree, and some opt for a combination of self-education through practice along with a variety of classes, lectures, and conferences. No matter how you choose to educate yourself,

the key to becoming a wildlife photographer is passion. You have to love the camera, the animals, and the thrill of the hunt for the perfect photo.

Here are a few tips:

- Be prepared to work freelance. A regular, nine-to-five job is out of the question.

- Build a portfolio of your work. As you improve, throw out the bad photos and keep adding better ones.

- Don't be ashamed to accept gigs taking wedding pictures or family photos. Everyone has to eat.

- Enter competitions.

- Get your work out there! Give your photos away to anyone or anyplace that will show them.

- Get your work reviewed and critiqued.

- Join a photography club or start a group with your friends.

- Know how to use your camera to get the most out of it.

- Listen and absorb what good photographers say at meetings or lectures.

- Once your photos are truly amazing, look for an agency to handle your work.

- Take pictures of a variety of subjects, including landscapes, close-ups, and portraits.

- Understand what makes for a great photo, like lighting, setting, and layout.

The National Aviary in Pennsylvania is the only independent indoor nonprofit zoo whose collection consists of only birds. Its mission is to "inspire respect for nature through an appreciation of birds." It has more than five hundred birds from 150 different species, including many that are rarely found in captivity. Its walk-through exhibits give visitors a chance to see these birds up close and personal.

SPOTLIGHT

Sir David Attenborough (1926—)
British Broadcaster and Naturalist

David Attenborough was born in England and spent his childhood roaming the campus of the University of Leicester where his father was the principal. He loved to collect fossils and rocks and studied everything he found living in the natural areas around his home. At the age of ten, he attended a lecture by British conservationist Grey Owl and was introduced to the idea that humans were damaging the planet and destroying wildlife and their habitats.

In college, Attenborough studied Geology and Zoology, earning a degree in Natural Science. After college, he worked as a children's textbook editor and then as a producer for the BBC (British Broadcasting Corporation), working on their nonfiction projects. His interest in natural science led to the production of the quiz show *Animal, Vegetable, Mineral?*, a series called *Animal Patterns*, and then the long-running series *Zoo Quest*, which aired on television from 1954 to 1963. He was the producer and presenter for *Zoo Quest*, which documented the capture of animals from around the world for the collections at the London Zoo. The series was very popular and it launched Attenborough's career as a nature documentarian.

Attenborough later worked for the BBC as a controller and then as the director of programming. In 1973, he resigned to pursue his writing and other projects. In 1979, his thirteen-part series *Life on Earth* aired and quickly became a hit. The quality of *Life on Earth* set the standard for all future wildlife documentaries and influenced generations of documentary filmmakers. *Life on Earth* was followed by *The Living Planet* in 1984 and in 1990 by *The Trials of Life*. Each series was a loving tribute to life on planet Earth.

Even into his 90s, Attenborough continues to devote his energy to the protection of wildlife and habitats around the world. He is the most traveled person in recorded history and the oldest person to visit the North Pole. He received over thirty honorary degrees; had several species of plants, insects, and birds named after him; and has been given many awards. From the dawn of the television era to the digital age, Sir David Attenborough has used his talents to spread the word about the plight of animals and the changing environment to anyone who would listen.

The Photo Ark

National Geographic photographer Joel Sartore is on a mission to document as many animals as he can before they go extinct. For over ten years, he has been their messenger to the world, saying, "We are here! We are here!" But some animals won't be here for long. Sartore's Photo Ark contains photos of over five thousand species. A favorite is the one he took of Toughie, a Rabb's fringe-limbed treefrog. Toughie is the last of his kind. At the age of nine, he's past his normal life expectancy. He's living at the Atlanta Botanical Garden, and when he dies, his species will be extinct.

Thousands of species like Toughie's are going extinct every day. Since the beginning of life on earth, there have been five mass extinctions. Today, scientists believe that the rate of plant and animal loss puts us in a sixth mass extinction. We are losing animals at a rate over one thousand times the normal extinction rate, possibly similar to 65 million years ago and the loss of the dinosaurs. Unstoppable hunting of large animals, climate change, loss of critical habitat, and explosive population growth (7.5 billion people!) is pounding away at our planet's biodiversity.

"Zoos often have the only populations of these animals—they're gone in the wild. And if it weren't for zoos, a lot of these species I shoot would be extinct by now," said Sartore. "I do take comfort in the fact that all is not lost by any means. In this country whooping crane, black-footed ferret, California condor, Mexican gray wolf, all those animals got down to fewer than two dozen, and they're all stable now—not in the best shape, but stable—and that just speaks volumes to the fact that people do care."[1]

||||||||||||||||||||||||||||||||||||||||||||||||||||||||||||||||||||||||||||||||||||||||||||||||||||||||||||||||||||||||

TOP DOG profile

Name: Amberley Snyder
Job: Cowgirl, Barrel Racer Roper, Motivational speaker

When did you first become interested in riding horses and decide to focus your career on rodeo competition?
I have loved horses for as long as I can remember. My mom had horses when she was younger but did not get to compete. When she saw my interest in horses she supported it and gave me the opportunities to begin riding them. I started riding at three years old

at the Ortega Riding Center in California. I remember taking my pony Gabby out, saddling and riding her. I wanted a pony because I wanted to be able to do everything by myself. Even at that age I was stubborn and independent. In my senior year of high school, I qualified for the National High School Finals Rodeo as well as for the Little Britches Finals, where I won the Finals and World All-Around title as well as was top 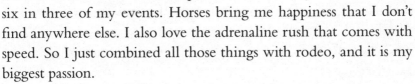 six in three of my events. Horses bring me happiness that I don't find anywhere else. I also love the adrenaline rush that comes with speed. So I just combined all those things with rodeo, and it is my biggest passion.

What education/training path did you take to get to where you are today?
I was able to do clinics with Ed Wright, Shirley Ankrum, and Sharon Camarillo. Plus, I have had a coach since I was younger, Stacy Glause. I've competed from the college level to the pro rodeo level. You learn to take the good with the bad, but always keep working for success.

I used to compete in barrel racing, pole bending, goat tying, and breakaway roping. I now compete in barrel racing and breakaway roping. I have pole bended again as well and plan to pick up team roping.

I am a person who truly believes in the "feel" of a horse. I don't think that is something you can teach or someone can show you. I think someone with natural horsemanship can really feel the horse beneath them. They can really understand where each foot is and how their body moves. By doing that, they have the capability to ask a horse to move and respond how they want.

What does it take to train a horse to be competitive?
A lot of time, patience, education, and effort. Winning on a horse you trained is more rewarding than winning on one someone else

has trained. When I was younger, I was so blessed with horses that knew the barrel pattern. As I got older, the skills I had gained from mentors and clinics were easily applied as I began training my own horses. When I was ten, I trained one from start to finish. It was a challenging, yet rewarding, experience. That was the first of many in my youth. My dad couldn't afford to buy finished barrel horses, so we would look for prospects, and it was my job to make them into something more valuable.

We went through a lot of horses before we got to Power. He was a challenging horse, as his attention span was so short and he was high-strung from the beginning. After the time and effort was put into him, he became the first barrel horse I wanted to keep. That horse became my "one in a million." He took care of me above himself every run.

In 2010, you had an accident that left you paralyzed from the waist down. How did that incident change the course of your career?

It postponed my goals for a little while, but has not changed them. When my accident happened, I sold my young horse at home because I was not sure if I would be able to do anything with him. I hoped to train my own horses one day, but wasn't sure how long that would take. My first thought was to look for horses that already knew the barrel pattern. We searched, but had trouble with this task in a few ways. I needed a horse that was a free runner, honest, and could figure out how to listen to my hands and my voice. Above all, I had to find someone who was willing to allow me to try their horses. This was the biggest challenge of all as not many were willing to allow me to ride.

I came to the conclusion that I was going to need to once again train my own. I first tried a young mare that was just started. She was talented but could not figure out how to respond without feeling my legs. That was when my boss, Lance Robinson, told me he would help me find a horse off his place. It took three tries to get to Legacy, but he [Lance] succeeded. The first time I got on Legacy, I knew I liked him. He could spin and stop and felt so athletic. My favorite part was the fire he had inside him. The first day he already knew to jump when I kissed at him. I took him home and the process began.

It took some time, but we figured out how to communicate with just my hands and my voice. He was ultra-sensitive when figuring out how to respond to me correctly, but it really came rather quickly. It was new for me and for him to learn a barrel pattern without the use of my legs. I am lucky this horse was more patient than I am or it might not have worked so quickly and smoothly. He continues to show me that even though I am strapped to my saddle, even though I cannot kick, even though I am in a wheelchair, I still have the ability to train a winning barrel horse. The process is different, a little slower and more challenging than before, but possible.

You were once president of the Utah Future Farmers of America. What did being a member of that organization mean to you?
Helping kids has been a passion of mine since being a part of the FFA. It is why I decided to pursue a career in agricultural education and school counseling. I'm attending Utah State University, pursuing a master's degree in school counseling. It is also why I became a motivational speaker.

What advice can you give students who are dreaming of competing in a rodeo?
My motto is, "There is no future in giving up!" Everyone faces obstacles. Everyone has hardships and hard times. Don't compare yourself to others around you. Face your obstacle in your own way with the support of others! It is okay to ask for help when you need it. But never, ever give up. If you have a dream you want to accomplish, then don't allow someone to tell you that you can't. Work hard and keep a positive attitude to keep moving forward.

What are some fun facts about yourself that aren't horse related?

I am a movie addict. I am almost constantly singing when I ride, even as I am walking up the alleyway to make a run. When I dream at night, I am always walking at some point. My favorite foods are steaks and potatoes.

9

Animals at Work

For thousands of years, animals have been used for work. From ancient times when donkeys, camels, and elephants carried people and supplies, to generations of horses and dogs accompanying soldiers during times of war, to modern cats, guinea pigs, and even goats and snakes being used for therapy, humans have used animals to meet their ever-changing needs. Today, animals are being used more and more for their great sense of smell, their agility and strength, and their comforting nature. This chapter will show you some of the areas where animals are being put to work each day.

Desert locusts sometimes join together to form gigantic, hungry swarms. According to *National Geographic*, "A desert locust swarm can be 460 square miles (1,200 square kilometers) in size and pack between 40 and 80 million locusts into less than half a square mile (one square kilometer). Each locust can eat its weight in plants each day, so a swarm of such size would eat 423 million pounds (192 million kilograms) of plants every day."[1] Not cool!

For Law Enforcement

Law enforcement has been working side by side with dogs for over one hundred years. In the late nineteenth century, England started using patrol dogs. The Belgians opened the first school for training patrol dogs in 1895. And in 1902, that school, located in the city of Ghent, had 120 police officers working with between fifty and sixty dogs, patrolling during the night shift from 10:00 PM to 6:00 AM. Within a decade, their program had expanded to Germany, Austria, Italy, and England.

It wasn't until the 1970s, following the Vietnam War, that the use of dogs for law enforcement became popular in the United States. Today, they are vital members of many police departments and other law enforcement agencies. Their fierce devotion to duty has earned them respect and the right to carry a badge. Since organizations started keeping records on their dogs in the mid-1960s, over 2,500 police and military dogs have died in the line of duty.

Law enforcement officers use dogs because of their size, intelligence, keen sense of smell, fierce devotion to their masters, and strong work ethic. The most common breed of dog used is the German shepherd because of its strength, intelligence, and unwavering obedience. The second most popular is the Belgian Malinois, known to be hardworking and intelligent, with great speed and agility.

Law enforcement agencies use specific dog breeds with special characteristics in the following areas:

🐾 for chasing and detaining a suspect—besides the two breeds mentioned above, police departments also use:
Akitas
Belgian sheepdogs
boxers
Doberman pinschers
rottweilers

🐾 for sniffing out illegal drugs or explosives in airports, train stations, major athletic events, political rallies, and anywhere there are huge crowds gathered, they use:
  basset hounds
  beagles
  English cocker spaniels
  foxhounds
  giant schnauzers

🐾 for long-distance sniffing to trail a lost person, hunt for a criminal, or find missing objects, they use:
  Australian shepherds
  bloodhounds
  coonhounds
  German shorthaired pointers
  Labrador retrievers

🐾 to detect the odor of decomposing bodies, or to find corpses or other human remains—these dogs' noses are so sensitive that they can smell a dead body under running water:
  beagles
  bloodhounds
  collies
  German shepherds
  golden retrievers

There are two ways detection dogs alert their handlers that they've found something. For a passive alert, commonly used for explosives, the dog sits to indicate it has detected something, and then waits until the handler finds the object the dog has smelled. For an aggressive alert, the dog scratches and barks where it smells a specific odor—this method is ideal to find concealed objects like drugs in airport luggage or bodies underground, but not for sensitive materials like explosives that could possibly detonate.

K-9 Officer

K-9 officers are part of a special task force within a police department. You don't get to have a K-9 partner as soon as you join a police department. It takes several years of experience before you get to pursue a K-9 officer position. The job of K-9 officer is the same as a regular officer. You still make traffic stops, assist in emergency calls, catch bad guys, and represent the police department at public events.

To become a K-9 officer, you should pursue a bachelor's degree in criminal justice, forensic science, or a related field. Not all law enforcement agencies require that you have a college degree. Be sure to check with the department you want to work for to verify its requirements. As part of the application process to become a police officer, you will go through these ten steps, probably in this order:

1. Take and pass a written exam.

2. Appear before an oral review board.

3. Appear before a citizen review board.

4. Take and pass a physical fitness test.

5. Pass a background investigation.

6. Take and pass a polygraph exam.

7. Undergo psychological testing.

8. Have an interview with the Chief of Police.

9. Pass a medical exam.

10. Pass a drug test.

Once you are hired by a police department, or a state or federal law enforcement agency, you will attend the police academy or the federal law enforcement training center. During the next three or more years on the force, you will gain experience and show your commanding officers and the administration that you are:

- able to handle stress appropriately

- able to understand animals

- accurate at report writing

- clear and precise when testifying in court

- friendly and comfortable talking to people

- living in a family willing to accept a dog

- an officer who thinks quickly and thoughtfully

- an officer who works with little supervision

- an officer with no citizen complaints

- an officer with no excessive use of force complaints

- open-minded and willing to learn

- a well-trained officer

Once you are chosen to become a canine officer, you will go through a canine training program to learn how to work with a dog. This training includes subjects like caring for your dog, safety protocols, crowd control, apprehending a suspect, and tracking. Together, you and your dog will go through obedience training and any job-specific training that you need.

Certification is available through the United States Police Canine Association. Dog handlers can be certified in basic areas like tracking, detection, searches, and apprehension. National training certifications are available in three levels, with the highest level given to those officers who have over fifteen years of experience.

Things to Consider before Becoming a K-9 Officer

- You will work mostly nights and weekends.

- Off hours are often interrupted for emergencies.

- You must care for the dog during your off time.

- You must find a suitable dog sitter when going on vacation.

- You must exercise your dog daily.

- You are responsible for your dog's food, medical care, and training.

- Dogs and their handlers can be an added liability for a police department. You must approach the job with integrity, restraint, and compassion.

Customs and Border Protection (CBP) Canine Program

Officers can work with dogs as part of the US Customs and Border Protection under the Department of Homeland Security. CBP

Decoys, sometimes called agitators or quarry, are an important part in training police dogs. These officers wear protective gear and pretend to be the bad guy, helping train the dog to approach, attack, and detain a suspect. A good decoy understands canine behavior language and can both stimulate the dog and reinforce good behaviors. Some departments look to their decoys to find future canine officers. Volunteering to be a decoy shows interest in working with dogs and provides valuable experience.

officers are on the front lines detecting and catching terrorists, stopping people from illegally entering the country, and finding and seizing illegal drugs, plants, and other goods that criminals try to bring into the country.

There are over 1,500 canine teams working for the US Customs and Border Patrol. It is the largest law enforcement canine program in the country. The CBP Canine Program has two training sites, the Canine Center El Paso in Texas and the Canine Center Front Royal in Virginia.

CBP Agriculture Canine Teams

Agriculture canine teams are part of the CBP, but are trained to detect harmful plant pests and foreign animal diseases and keep them from entering the United States. Dogs use their sensitive noses and are trained to alert on specific odors, like those coming from certain fruits, vegetables, plants, and meat products, and from pests like snails. Beagles are the dog of choice to work in airports because of their keen sense of smell, non-threatening size, high food drive, and gentle disposition with the public. Over one hundred agriculture canine teams work at border crossings, airport terminals, cruise terminals, cargo warehouses, and mail facilities that process international passengers and cargo. Teams are trained at the USDA's National Detector Dog Training Center in Atlanta, Georgia. This is a separate training program from the CBP Canine Program.

|||||||||||||||||||||||||||||||||||||||||||||||||||||||||||||||||||||||||||||||||||||||||||||||||||||||||||||||||||

TOP DOG *profile*

Name: Janice Baker, DVM
Job: Lieutenant Colonel, Commander of Veterinary Unit in the US Army Reserve, Owner and Director of Research and Development at Veterinary Tactical Group

When did you first become interested in working with animals and decide to make it the focus of your career?
Like a lot of people, I knew from early childhood that I wanted to work with animals. I grew up with horse racing, and my first paid job was cleaning stalls and grooming racehorses. I was always fascinated with the veterinarians and their work when they came to the barns, and I knew that eventually that's what I wanted to do.

What education/work path did you take to get to your current position?
I dropped out of the eighth grade to work with horses because I had trouble in school, and I did not attend high school. However, I loved learning and took some courses by correspondence until I could earn my high school equivalency. It took a few years to get on track, but then I attended community college to try to earn a degree as a veterinary technician. One of our instructors recognized the enthusiasm and motivation in another student and me and told us that we would never be happy as technicians and that we needed to shoot for veterinary school. Eventually, we transferred to university and then were accepted to veterinary school. I am so thankful for that

encouragement, because with my lack of high school background, I would never have thought it possible to become a veterinarian. I attended the University of California, Davis, graduating as a doctor of veterinary medicine in 1999. Following graduation, I completed an internship at North Carolina State University in equine field service with the intention of becoming a specialist in horse medicine.

Why did you decide to join the US Army Veterinary Corps instead of going into private practice after veterinary school?

After my internship, I joined the US Army Veterinary Corps to help pay off the cost of school. That was right before 9/11 [terrorist attacks in the United States on September 11, 2001], and my first duty station was in Washington, DC, right next to the Pentagon. Following 9/11, most of my duties involved caring for working dogs, and I really fell in love with them. Since then, I've dedicated my entire career to working dogs.

You were deployed to Iraq and Afghanistan. Describe your work during those missions and the animals you worked with.

In Iraq and Afghanistan, I cared for military working dogs at several bases across both countries. My job was to travel around and make sure the other veterinarians and canine handlers had everything they needed to provide top-notch care for the dogs. That might include special medications, specialized canine first aid kits for the handlers, or training for medics, handlers, and veterinary personnel in case a dog was injured in the line of duty.

Explain what a high-risk tactical canine operation is and how you train handlers and their canines to work safely.

A "high-risk" canine operation is any mission where injury is more likely to occur to either humans or dogs. This may mean entering an unstable structure after an earthquake, working during very hot or very cold weather, or where there are other people trying to do harm to the handler or dog, such as in military or police work.

Treating injured dogs in these conditions is different than treating them in a clinic. We train the handlers to provide emergency care in complete darkness, in the back of moving vehicles or helicopters, and to do some tasks usually reserved for trained veterinarians, since it may be hours to days before they reach veterinary care. We spend a lot of time working with them to prevent injuries and illness, too, like teaching them how to increase their dogs' physical fitness, or get them used to being handled by medics who may have to treat them in the field.

Describe the working dog research projects you are conducting.

We are currently working on a project to measure body temperature changes in dogs exercising at high altitudes and in cold temperatures. We get pretty cold, but the dogs seem to love it! This study will eventually help us understand the physical abilities of dogs, such as search and rescue dogs or police dogs, that have to work high in the mountains. We are also working on a study of injuries to police dogs within the United States. For this study, we are looking at cases that have already happened and trying to find common things about the case that increase or decrease the chances of survival, as well as how the cases were handled forensically—yes, that is CSI [crime scene investigation] for police dogs!

What tips would you give kids who are interested in pursuing a career working with animals in law enforcement or the military?

Working with animals is not limited to just one area of interest. It can involve science and math, psychology, teaching, business management, criminal justice, and even art. You can take your personal interests and talents and use them to work with animals in many ways. Get to know your local K-9 unit, veterinary clinics, and dog or horse trainers. Get involved with farming and agricultural clubs. Or, look for other types of animal activities you really enjoy.

Make sure to study hard in school. Whatever you do with animals, you need to be able to think, write, and communicate clearly, whether it's instructions to a dog owner on pet care after surgery, teaching canine first aid to handlers, writing police reports, or teaching at a veterinary school.

What is your favorite animal and why?

My favorite animal to work on in veterinary medicine is the dog, of course! But I am also a big cat lover and have cats at home for my personal pets. It's a toss-up between cats and dogs. Dogs are so loyal and sincere. Cats seem to act mysterious, and like furry royalty they hide that they are just little goofballs inside. They keep me laughing after a hard day's work!

For the Military

Dogs have been in combat with US soldiers during every major conflict since the Revolutionary War. They were companions, mascots, and messengers during the Civil War and the Spanish-American War. During World War I, a few served in the trenches of France. During World War II, the first K-9 Corps was established. About eighteen thousand dogs went through the army's twelve-week basic training, and about ten thousand were deployed for active duty. During the heaviest fighting, in 1943 and 1944, fifteen dog platoons served in the European and Asian theaters. During WWII, the Korean War, and the Vietnam War, they were guard dogs, patrol dogs, and scouts.

SPOTLIGHT

Sergeant Stubby (ca. 1916–1926), Hero of WWI, Grandfather of the American War Dog

In 1917, an army private named J. Robert Conroy was combat training on the Yale University campus when he found a tiny puppy with a stub for a tail. The dog, named Stubby, soon became the mascot of the 102nd Infantry, 26th Yankee Division. He learned all the bugle calls, followed through the combat drills, and even learned to salute his commanding officer by putting his right paw up to his right eyebrow.

When it was time to deploy overseas, Conroy smuggled Stubby aboard the *USS Minnesota* by hiding him in the coal bin. As Conroy tried to sneak Stubby off the ship in France, his commanding officer spotted him. Conroy was allowed to keep Stubby with him after the officer got an instantly recognizable salute from the dog.

Stubby served in seventeen battles and was injured several times. He also encountered poisonous gas. His sensitivity to the gas helped him save the lives of his entire company by alerting them when he smelled gas during an attack. He also helped rescue wounded soldiers by listening for their cries, finding them, and then barking to alert the paramedics. He even helped capture a German spy by finding him hiding in a bush and sounding the alarm. His bravery earned him the rank of sergeant, the first dog to be given a rank in the US Armed Forces.

After the war, he was made a lifetime member of the American Legion, the Red Cross, and the YMCA. Newspapers across the country told his story, and he met with three sitting United States Presidents: Woodrow Wilson, Warren G. Harding, and Calvin Coolidge.

Stubby was awarded several medals for bravery, including the Purple Heart. He died in 1926. His body was preserved and is on display at the Smithsonian Museum in Washington, DC.

Military working dogs (MWDs) and their handlers get intensive training at a cost of $20,000 to $40,000 per dog. This cost, plus the time and effort it takes to train them, means that MWDs are valuable and well-cared-for animals. When stationed in Iraq and Afghanistan, these modern war dogs carry specialized equipment. They wear vests that protect them from bullets and knife attacks. They carry global positioning system (GPS) devices and infrared night-sight cameras. And many wear "doggles," which are special canine goggles that protect their eyes from blowing sand.

To work as a military dog handler, you must first join one of the branches of the military. This is usually a four-year commitment. Talk to a recruiter from each branch to find out how to get into their specific war dog programs. Joining the military requires a high school diploma or GED. You also must be a US citizen or permanent resident alien, in good physical condition, and between seventeen and thirty-five years old.

Robby's Law, passed by President Bill Clinton in 2000, allows handlers and their families the chance to adopt their military dogs when their service is over. If the handler doesn't adopt the dog, it is offered to law enforcement and then to adoptive families. The law is named after a dog whose handler tried to adopt him, but the military euthanized him instead.
This law changes the status of retired military dogs from obsolete equipment to honored veterans.

Military dogs can be trained for either a single purpose or a dual purpose. Single-purpose dogs have one job to do. A list of specialized jobs is below.

- ❧ Explosive detector dogs are used in all branches of the military by the military police.

- ❧ Narcotics detector dogs are used in all branches of the military by the military police.

- ❧ Specialized search dogs are trained to work off leash at long distances to find explosives. They are not used in the air force or the navy.

- ❧ Combat tracker dogs are trained to track down enemies who have had contact with explosives. They are used by the marine corps only.

- ❧ Mine detection dogs are trained to find buried mines and artillery. They are used by the army only.

Dual-purpose dogs can be used both to detect and to patrol. A list of specialized jobs is below.

- ❧ Patrol explosive detector dogs are used by the military police and other law enforcement in all branches of service. They sniff out bombs, perform scouting duties, and do patrol work.

- ❧ Patrol narcotics detector dogs are used to sniff out drugs as well as for scouting and patrol duties. They are used in the army, navy, air force, and marine corps.

- ❧ Multi-purpose canines are used by special operations personnel. These dogs do what the first two groups do, plus much more. They are super-high-drive dogs that can parachute out of planes. They wear specialized equipment and can work at a distance from their handlers. They are resilient, strong, and unflappable—ready for any challenge. The Navy SEALS used a Belgian Malinois named Cairo during their raid on Osama Bin Laden in 2013.

* Central Intelligence Agency (CIA) K-9 Corps are used to guard the people who work for the CIA. They travel and often work with other law enforcement teams. They also work on special assignments, like guarding at the Super Bowl or other high-profile events.

Chips, a shepherd-collie-husky mix, was the most famous and decorated sentry dog in World War II, receiving the Silver Star, the Distinguished Service Cross, and the Purple Heart. His acts of bravery included capturing fourteen enemy soldiers in the invasion of Sicily, during which he was wounded flushing out four soldiers from a machine gun nest. After Chips, the military decided to no longer award these medals to warrior dogs, though dogs can still receive an honorary purple heart.

Special Service

According to the Americans with Disabilities Act, a service animal is a dog that is individually trained to perform tasks for a person with a disability, including "guiding people who are blind, alerting people who are deaf, pulling a wheelchair, alerting and protecting a person who is having a seizure, reminding a person with mental illness to take prescribed medications, calming a person with Post Traumatic Stress Disorder (PTSD) during an anxiety attack, or performing other duties."[2] Service animals are working animals, not pets.

Here are a few areas where specially trained animals are needed. If any of them interest you, you should follow the animal trainer career path:

- anxiety therapy dogs

- cancer-sniffing dogs

- companion dogs for the mentally ill

- diabetic alert dogs

- guide dogs for the blind

- guide dogs for the deaf

- wheelchair assistance dogs

- seizure alert dogs

||||||||||||||||||||||||||||||||||||||||||||||||||||||||||||||||||||||||||||||||||||||||||||||||||||||||||||

Name: Julia Saunders
Age: 17
Job (when not studying!): Guide Dog Puppy Raiser for Southeastern Guide Dogs

When did you first discover your love for dogs, and how did you decide that helping raise guide dogs was what you wanted to do?
I have always loved dogs, and I was interested in doing some community service. I was assigned a year-long project in eighth grade and I knew I wanted to raise a guide dog for that assignment. I had to talk my parents into it. But, since my older brother was

going off to college that September, they agreed. My mom and I attended puppy-raiser meetings the summer between my seventh- and eighth-grade years of middle school. Then we had a home visit and a background check. I was so excited when we got the call to pick up a little black Labrador retriever named Sarah. She was named by the local chapter of the University of Pennsylvania Alumni Club. Groups and individuals donate money to name a dog since Southeastern is nonprofit and supported completely by donations.

Describe your volunteer organization.
I am a volunteer puppy raiser for Southeastern Guide Dogs, Inc., in Palmetto, Florida. We raise guide dogs for blind adults age eighteen and older. Dogs that do not qualify as guide dogs can be considered for our veteran service dogs program, providing dogs for veterans with PTSD. We also place dogs in medical facilities, police departments, fire departments, and arson programs. Some of our dogs become pets for blind children, to get them used to dogs so they can handle a service dog when they are old enough.

Describe the dogs you have raised and your experiences with them.
We got Sarah, a black Labrador retriever, when she was sixteen weeks old and kept her until she was sixteen months old. She went to school with me and to all of my classes. Once, she fell asleep in my history class and started snoring so loud the teacher had to stop class. She went to restaurants and shopping centers with us, and to puppy-raiser meetings. I even took her on a plane to Chicago to visit relatives. She was so good the person sitting next to us didn't even know there was a dog under my feet.

Sarah was sassy. She wouldn't do something if she didn't want to. Luckily, when she went "in for training" (IFT) to Guide Dog University, her trainers were able to channel that energy into service work. She was matched as a guide with a wonderful woman named Dottie Langham from Georgia. The trainers were waiting for someone like Dottie to come along who would be a great handler for Sarah. She is completely blind and depends on Sarah for her safety. We keep in close touch with Sarah. She is doing a great job as a guide and even helping Dottie teach a little blind girl braille at a school near their home.

We picked up our second dog, Blue, just before Sarah went off to formal training. He was the last member of his litter in the puppy kennel. He really needed a raiser, so we volunteered. When the puppies are born in the kennel they receive a different color collar depending on their birth order. He had a blue collar. By the time we took him home, he was answering to the name Blue, so we kept that name. Blue was a ball of energy. He is a beautiful white lab who loves all people. Blue went to baseball games at Tropicana Field to see the Tampa Bay Rays, and he also went to school with me sometimes. All of the kids in my middle school knew that when my dogs had their official cape on, they weren't allowed to pet them. That means they are "working." The coats or capes are used to help the dogs get used to having something on their backs so they are comfortable with the harness when they go in for training. Blue was a perfect puppy at our meetings, and he knew all of his commands when he went IFT. But, after a few months in the training kennel, we got a call that he had developed a fear of thunderstorms. In Florida, we have lots of rain and storms, mostly in the summer. That fear was enough to have him released from the guide dog program and the other options at Southeastern. We adopted Blue and he is now our family pet. He still hates storms, but he loves EVERYBODY.

When Blue went IFT, we picked up a little black lab named Emerald. We called her Emmie. She was the runt of her litter and had some problems growing. She was beautiful and reminded us so much of our Sarah. She was the only one of our puppies who liked swimming. Once she got used to the pool, we couldn't get her out of it! She was sweet and tried hard to please us. But, she started to develop some serious food allergies. She had a lot of medical tests and always seemed to have an upset tummy. Southeastern decided she had to be "career changed." She was adopted by a really great family from Alabama with two small kids.

After Emmie we got a black lab named Max. Max liked to put everything in his mouth—everything! He chewed on our furniture, our walls, our rugs, and our arms and legs. He was so funny and so smart. Max was a very high-energy puppy. The only problem was, Blue was high energy too. The two of them would play like crazy all day and never settle down. We started to worry that if Max stayed in our home with Blue, he might never be able to calm down enough for guide work. So, Max went to another puppy raiser called a "finisher." Earlier this year, Max was matched as a veteran's service dog.

Our fifth dog was Hannah. She was what they call at Southeastern my "heart" dog. I love her so much. She was a sweet and tiny yellow lab who made us laugh every day. Hannah was smart and loved to sleep at our feet, always touching us. She was so much fun to have around the house, and she and Blue got along so well. Hannah went IFT to Guide Dog University in January of this year (2016). So far, her training reports have been excellent, and it seems like she might become a guide dog.

A couple months after Hannah went in, we picked up our sixth guide dog puppy. Her name is Hillary. She is a cute little yellow lab with lots of personality. She loves Blue, and he is so happy to have another playmate in the house. She just graduated from puppy kindergarten, and she is ready to begin wearing her big-girl cape and going on outings very soon. I can't wait to bring her to high school with me.

What is the process you use for raising a puppy?
Puppy raisers are required to housebreak their puppies and teach them basic obedience. In puppy kindergarten we teach them how

to go potty on command. We tell them to "busy" and give them just enough leash to go where we want, and they learn to do their business right there. That's important because blind people need to know where their dogs go "busy" so they can pick it up.

The puppies need to learn good house manners (no getting on furniture, counter surfing, or jumping on people) and they need to learn to look to their raiser for directions. We use treat training and reward them for doing what we ask them to do. We have trainers that help us teach them basic commands like sit, let's go, heel, stay, and come. We teach them to sit at doors and stairs to warn their future blind handler what's ahead of them. We also help them learn to turn left and right on command. Our main job, though, is socializing the puppies and helping them to learn about the world and all its sounds and sights. We have two required puppy meetings a month where we take the puppies out as a group to get different exposures. We go to the local fire station, the beach, the boardwalk, the gymnasium, and the movie theater. We take them on city buses and to concerts. Our goal is to help the puppies become confident guide dogs. Some of the puppies take longer to get comfortable with things like loud noises, so we help each puppy at their own pace.

How do you handle giving up a puppy that you have grown to love?

Everyone always asks, "How can you give up the puppy after a year?" Yes. It's hard. Giving up Sarah was probably the hardest thing I ever did. I cried every time I thought about her in the kennel. But, the day I met

Dottie, I knew that she had a bigger purpose and that even though I LOVED Sarah, Dottie NEEDED Sarah. It never gets easier when you have to say goodbye. But now I know how exciting it can be to see what career the dogs end up with. I can't wait to hear about Max and all his adventures as a veteran's service dog. And I have a feeling Hannah is going to make a very special guide dog. I can hardly wait to see her little head tilt when I see her again on Puppy Raiser Day.

Where do you see yourself in ten years?
I am finishing my junior year of high school and looking at colleges. I have looked at a school near where Sarah lives in Georgia that I like a lot. I also am looking at schools where I could possibly raise a guide dog while attending college classes. I like talking to people and I like doing things to help people. I am hoping to get involved in communications, maybe for a nonprofit like Southeastern.

Other Working Animals

African giant pouched rats can be trained to sniff out landmines and help diagnose tuberculosis by smelling it inside a patient. They are smart and calm, and their eight-year lifespan makes them very useful. Native to sub-saharan Africa, they are adaptable and are being used in Thailand, Vietnam, and Cambodia.

Capuchin monkeys can be trained to help people with disabilities perform manual tasks like picking up items, turning knobs, and flipping switches. They can even turn the pages of a book.

Dolphins assist people with autism, Down syndrome, and cerebral palsy by helping them improve their body movements, speech and language skills, and attention spans. The US Navy has over eighty bottlenose dolphins that are trained to locate underwater mines, watch for and alert their handlers if an enemy swimmer is in the water, and guard vessels and sea ports. The navy also has about fifty trained sea lions.

Eagles are trained to swoop down on drones, grasp them in their talons, and bring them to the ground without hurting nearby humans or themselves in the process. These strong and intelligent birds are used by law enforcement agencies around the world as part of their anti-terrorism and anti-crime efforts.

Ferrets are used to pull digital or electrical wires through tunnels or tubes. They also help detect breaks or damage in underground network wires by carrying microchips fastened to the little jackets that they wear.

Horses can help with physical, occupational, and speech-language therapy. They are also used to help people with social, mental health, and behavior problems. They are used to herd cattle and for travel in areas where a vehicle cannot go.

Manatees and hippopotamuses are used to control invasive water hyacinth in California's Sacramento–San Joaquin Delta. Each animal can eat two hundred to three hundred pounds of vegetation a day.

Miniature horses can be trained to guide the blind. They can also pull wheelchairs or walk alongside and support a person with Parkinson's disease.

Taxonomist Name Game

Below is an A to Z list of some of the most amazing creatures on earth! Using the internet (with your parents' permission), pretend that you are a taxonomist, a biologist that gives names to groups of organisms. Put the first name in your search engine and find a picture of the animal. You know what other scientists have named it, but what would *you* name it? After choosing a new name, try to describe it, using the most precise words possible. Don't hesitate to grab a thesaurus. When you are finished with the first, move on to the others. When you have completed the entire list, you will understand the wonderful diversity of earth's creatures—and how hard it is to describe and name new species.

1. Aye-aye

2. Blob fish

3. Coconut crab

4. Dumbo octopus

5. Dugong

6. Emperor tamarin

7. Fried egg jellyfish

8. Goblin shark

9. Hummingbird hawk-moth

10. Ice cream cone worm

11. Japanese spider crab

12. Komondor dog

13. Leafy seadragon

14. Mantis shrimp

15. Naked mole rat

16. Okapi

17. Pink fairy armadillo

18. Quetzal

19. Red-lipped batfish

20. Star-nosed mole

21. Tasseled wobbegong

22. *Umbonia* spinosa

23. Venezuelan poodle moth

24. *Wunderpus photogenicus*

25. X-ray tetra

26. Yeti crab

27. Zebra duiker

Animals and Research

Working with animals as a scientist or researcher is a huge field. There are many opportunities no matter what area interests you. To work with animals and conduct research, you will need a minimum of a bachelor's degree, but for most positions, and to advance in the career, a master's degree and PhD will be required. While in high school, don't shy away from classes like biology, botany, ecology, and chemistry. They will teach you the importance of the scientific method and the best ways to keep records and present your data to other scientists.

Animal Science

If you are interested in farm animal research, then pursuing a degree in animal science might be right for you. There are many jobs available in this field, covering a wide range of animals. Whether you earn a bachelor's degree or go on for a master's degree or doctorate, this is a growing field and the jobs won't be disappearing anytime soon. People need to be fed, and animal science will help make that happen as the number of people on earth continues to increase.

Animal science, in the past called animal husbandry, is the study of animals that are under the control of humans. It includes animals raised for food, like cattle, pigs, and sheep, and animals

Tardigrades, or water bears, are microscopic creatures with amazing survival abilities. They can withstand temperatures from almost absolute zero to above the boiling point of water, the vacuum of space, and solar radiation, and they can go for more than ten years without food or water. They can even survive being frozen for thirty years! Billions of these hard-to-kill creatures exist all over the planet. Although they can endure harsh conditions, they prefer living in moss, dirt, or sand.

raised for their products, like chickens for eggs, goats and alpacas for fiber, and dairy cattle for milk. The animal food industry is one of the largest and most important industries in the United States.

Name: Helena Brown
Age: 14
Job (when not studying!): Future Herpetologist

When did you first discover your love for animals and decide that you wanted to work with them?
I have always loved animals and science from a young age. I first decided that I wanted to work with animals when I was about ten or eleven years old. This was when I was given my first pet, a Russian tortoise. I began researching reptiles and became more and more interested in herpetology [the study of amphibians and reptiles]. I joined the San Diego Turtle and Tortoise Society

(SDTTS), and that was pretty much when I decided that I wanted to work in the science field.

Describe your experiences with the San Diego Zoo Corps.
This is my first session in Zoo Corps. It has been an amazing experience for me. Zoo Corps has taught me presentation and speaking skills as well as information about a variety of animals, habitats, and environmental conservation.

You are interested in herpetology. Explain what that is and what you're doing now.
Herpetology is the study of reptiles and my favorite type of science. I am currently a member of the SDTTS and have four reptiles in my care. I take care of a Chinese water dragon and three desert tortoises. The tortoises are currently dormant, but during the warmer months they require daily care. They are given various amounts of food and supplements, which are hidden around their enclosure for enrichment purposes. They also have multiple water bowls that need daily cleaning and refilling. I let them roam about in our backyard, supervised, so they get plenty of exercise and play time.

The Chinese water dragon also requires daily water changing and cleaning, but he is not fed as often. He is usually fed two to three times a week with a diet consisting of mealworms, earthworms, and various sorts of vegetables and fruits. For enrichment, there are various toys introduced and interchanged every once in a while. His places for basking in the sun are also interchanged.

Why are you so passionate about conservation?
I have always been involved in conservation; my family recycles and conserves in multiple ways. However, it was not until I became a member of Zoo Corps that I became more proactive and passionate about it. I have learned how important it really is.

I hope to raise awareness about the importance of conservation both through Zoo Corps and on my own.

One of my favorite quotes is from Dr. Dame Daphne Sheldrick, who is a Kenyan author and conservationist. She said, "Saving wildlife and wilderness is the responsibility of all thinking people. Greed and personal gain must not be permitted to decimate, despoil and destroy the earth's irreplaceable treasure, for its existence is essential to the human spirit and the well-being of the earth as a whole. All life has just one home—the earth—and we as the dominant species must take care of it."

I am in complete agreement with Dr. Sheldrick. Although all of earth's natural resources need to be conserved, my main concern and passion is focused on habitat restoration. Habitat destruction is broadly considered to be the primary threat to wildlife around the world; [it] is caused by humans destroying natural habitats to build random shopping centers or other developments.

Another reason why so many animals are in trouble is because of illegal poaching and hunting. Now, as the fairly average person, you can do so much to help the problems concerning poaching or habitat destruction by just conserving and recycling. Conservation helps to preserve a lot of elements that play big roles in the endangerment of animals. One such element would be colton, which is commonly found in cell phones. Colton is mined in the eastern portion of the Democratic Republic of the Congo, which is also primary gorilla habitat. When miners harvest the ore, not only do they disrupt the habitat and leave behind "human germs," but they also create roads for poachers and bush meat hunters. However, if people recycled their cell phones, the demand for colton would decrease dramatically, which in turn would help preserve the gorilla and its natural habitat. It is a very similar situation for many other minerals and substances, such as aluminum, paper, bauxite, and plastic.

What books and magazines do you enjoy?
I love reading, especially historical fiction and science fiction. I also look forward to my monthly magazines from SDTTS and *ZOONOOZ*.

What is your favorite animal and why?

My favorite animal is the Komodo dragon because it is incredibly powerful and very interesting to study. One cool fact about the Komodo dragon is that it is only found in certain places in Indonesia. The Komodo dragon is also endangered and is supported by organizations such as the San Diego Zoo.

Where do you see yourself in the future?

I am planning to pursue some of Zoo Corps' educational opportunities. I hope to be chosen for another session with them. In addition, the Zoological Society of San Diego has high school internships and college fellowship programs in various fields of work. Next year, the summer when I am 16 years old, I will be applying for any job at the San Diego Zoo/Safari Park that is available. I have met many inspiring people who work within the Zoological Society. I hope that by being involved there, it may lead to more opportunities for me in the future. After that, I plan on going to college and getting a degree in biology with a focus on herpetology and conservation.

Animal Science Areas of Study

- animal behavior and welfare

- animal health and pre-veterinary medicine

- animal nutrition

- animal waste disposal

- disease control

- food production

- genetics

- livestock business management

- microbiology

Where Animal Scientists Work

- animal breeding companies

- animal feed manufacturing companies

- colleges and universities as teachers and researchers

- consulting firms

- environmental regulatory agencies

- farms and ranches

- federal and state governments

- food processing companies

- health management and disease control agencies

- industrial food research companies

- international agencies

- meat packers

- media companies, as writers and public speakers

- organizations like the National Cattlemen's Association, National Pork Producers Council, or the National Dairy Herd Improvement Association

- pharmaceutical companies

- private corporations

- processing, handling, and quality-control agencies

Temple Grandin was diagnosed with brain damage at the age of two. It wasn't until she was an adult that she received her true diagnosis of autism. Even with the disorder, she graduated from college and went on to complete a master's degree and a doctoral degree in animal science. Having a good education helped her become one of the first people to share what it was like to live with autism.

Feelings of anxiety in everyday life led her to focus her career on the humane processing of livestock. She studied animal behavior extensively and then designed corrals that reduced the animals' stress when they were being led to slaughter. Today, despite her disorder, she designs facilities for Burger King, McDonald's, and many other large meat processing companies. She also teaches animal science at Colorado State University and is a champion for the rights of people with autism.

Wildlife Biologists

Wildlife biologists are scientists who observe wildlife in natural habitats to help determine an animal's role in the ecosystem and food chain, whether or not there are adequate numbers for that species' health, and how human actions are affecting it. Most wildlife biologists spend a lot of time outdoors, observing behaviors and recording activities like group interactions, food intake, and breeding and birth cycles. The rest of their time is spent in the laboratory, studying their data. Wildlife biologists specialize in a specific area or on a specific species.

These tasks are common to most wildlife biologists:

- advocate for animals and their habitat protection

- keep accurate records and collect samples

- plan and execute observation field trips

- provide expert testimony when needed

- write reports to document findings

- work with other scientists who are doing complimentary research

- work with others to monitor animals and their habitats

Bird Biologists

Aviculturist is a broad term for anyone who keeps and breeds birds in captivity. They may raise small flocks of chickens as a hobby; raise chickens, ostriches, or emus on farms; or conduct bird research for zoos and universities. The education requirements change depending on the area the aviculturist decides to pursue.

Ornithologists study birds. They know about bird anatomy, habitats, migration patterns, diets, and reproduction. Some specialize in

As attitudes change and people become more aware of the misuse and abuse of animals, the increase in animal extinctions, and the depth of some animals' comprehension of the world in which they live, there is increasing pressure on organizations to change or stop the way they use animals for profit or research. Here are four of the most recent animal welfare developments:

1. In May 2015, Harvard Medical School stopped using primates for medical research and closed its New England Primate Research Center. It sent approximately two thousand primates to other centers.

2. In March 2016, SeaWorld announced that it will stop breeding orcas in captivity. This policy will eventually lead to the end of whale shows at the parks. SeaWorld will still have whales, but its focus will be on rescue and conservation.

3. In May 2016, Ringling Bros. and Barnum & Baily circus discontinued using Asian elephants in performances. Their last show was in Providence, Rhode Island. The animals retired to the Ringling Bros. Center for Elephant Conservation in Florida.

4. By 2020, the National Aquarium in Baltimore will move its bottlenose dolphins to a dolphin sanctuary in the ocean where they will be protected but can live out their lives in a natural habitat.

areas like bird songs, flight patterns, and diseases, and some focus on a specific species or category like scavengers or predators.

No college offers a specific degree in ornithology. To become an ornithologist, you need a bachelor's degree in a scientific field like biology, wildlife biology, or zoology. After that, you will need one or more master's degrees with course work in the bird-related subjects that interest you. If you want to teach at a college or university, or conduct research, plan to get a doctoral degree.

Most ornithologists are employed at colleges or universities, by agencies in the state or federal government, or by organizations like zoos, aquariums, or wildlife refuges. Many ornithologists do not work exclusively with birds. They may focus on birds but work as ecologists, geneticists, wildlife biologists, land managers, teachers, researchers, outdoor educators, or tour leaders.

The elephant bird, a species hunted to extinction in the seventeenth century, lived in Madagascar, could grow to be ten feet tall, and weighed half a ton. Their eggs—the largest in the world—were over a foot long and could hold one hundred chicken eggs inside them! Approximately twenty-five fossilized and semi-fossilized elephant bird eggs still exist. Scientists have extracted DNA from one of these eggs, kindling hope that one day the elephant bird could be brought back.

What Ornithologists Do

- advocate for all birds, especially those that are endangered

- collect and analyze sound recordings of birds

- collect data and keep detailed records

- conduct studies to determine changes in bird populations, including ways they adapt to changing environments and how they adapt to diseases

- create bird management plans

- manage endangered species by working with conservation, protection, and rehabilitation organizations

- monitor migration trends

- study birds in their natural habitat

- use computer modeling software to follow population changes

- write scientific reports and journal articles

Fish Biologists

Ichthyology is the study of fishes, also called fish science. It is a specific part of zoology that focuses on around twenty thousand species of fish, which include osteichthyans (those with boney skeletons), chondrichthyans (those with skeletons made of cartilage instead of bone), and agnathans (primitive fishes without jaws).

If you want a career working with fishes, then you need to know the difference between a marine biologist and an aquatic biologist. Pay attention! Knowing this will make you seem really smart. Marine biologists work with fishes that live in saltwater, in the seas or oceans. Aquatic biologists work with fishes that live in freshwater, like lakes, streams, and rivers.

||||||||||||||||||||||||||||||||||||||||||||||||||||||||||||||||||||||||||||||||||||||||||||

TOP DOG *profile*

Name: John Easterbrooks
Job: Regional Fish Program Manager for the Washington Department of Fish and Wildlife

When did you first become interested in working with fishes and decide to make it the focus of your career?

I was an undergraduate forestry/wildlife student at the University of Maine (Orono) in the early 1970s. While researching career opportunities, I found that there were more jobs in fishery management/science than in wildlife (birds, mammals). Besides that, I always loved fish and fishing as a boy. For two summers while in Maine (before and after my college senior year), I worked for the Maine Department of Inland Fisheries and Game as a fisheries research technician on several very interesting field studies. I worked with professional fish biologists who mentored and encouraged me. We worked with charismatic gamefish species like sea-run Atlantic salmon, brook trout, landlocked salmon, Sunapee trout, lake trout, and smallmouth bass to name a few. That was it! I was "hooked" on a career in fisheries.

What education/work path did you take to get to your current position?

I knew I wanted to study forestry, wildlife, and/or fisheries in college, so I was motivated to be a good math and science student in high school. After graduating with a BS degree in wildlife management from the University of Maine and working for the equivalent of two full years for the Maine Fish and Game Department as a scientific technician, I decided to pursue a master of science (MS) degree in fishery resource management. I was motivated by a lack of permanent fish biologist jobs in the New England states at that time (1975), and an understanding that an advanced degree would lead to more and better permanent career opportunities. So, I enrolled as an MS student at the University of Idaho (Moscow) and completed my degree in 1981. But before finishing my thesis, I accepted an entry-level fish biologist job with the Washington Department of Fisheries in Olympia, Washington, in 1978. I was married, and our oldest daughter, Shannon, was a year old, so I jumped at the opportunity to get started on my professional career and provide for my young family. During my first five years, I worked on instream flow studies for salmon and steelhead, and on evaluating the impact of major hydroelectric projects.

Then, in 1983, we moved east of the Cascade Mountains so I could work as the lead for the Yakima [Fish] Screen Shop (YSS). For over sixteen years, my YSS team designed, constructed, installed, and maintained fish screens and fish bypass systems on surface water diversions. We worked on small to very large irrigation diversions in the semi-arid Yakima Basin, which is a major agricultural area (five hundred thousand irrigated acres) called the "fruit bowl of the nation." Fish screens/bypasses protect juvenile salmon, steelhead, and resident fishes from being diverted from rivers and creeks and being killed. We also maintained a number of small fish ladders in central Washington. During those years, I was a senior fish biologist and spent a lot of time working in the field with my crew of metal fabricators and construction craftsmen, designing and building fish screen facilities that had an immediate survival benefit for the fish. This tangible, on-the-ground work was the most fun I have had during my career.

In 1999, I left the Yakima Screen Shop and accepted a promotion to my current position as the regional fish program manager for Southcentral Washington. I manage district fish biologists (fish and fishery management) and several hatcheries that produce salmon, steelhead, resident trout, and warm-water species for stocking in rivers and lakes. Thirty-eight years later, I am still working for the Department of Fisheries, which merged with the Department of Game in 1994, creating the existing agency, the Washington Department of Fish and Wildlife.

Describe your job and what a normal day might look like for you.
I am a senior manager now and spend most of my time in the office behind a computer, managing people, budgets, etc. or

going to meetings. However, my thirty-six years of experience working fish and water management issues in the Yakima Basin means I still get to spend a good part of my time on strategic or tactical planning. I secure funding and implement plans to restore or increase salmon, steelhead, bull trout, and Pacific lamprey populations and work with other government agencies (federal, state, county) and native American tribes, mainly the Yakama Nation. Not much fieldwork, but still very satisfying when we are successful making an improvement (significant or even incremental) that advances fish recovery and allows us to provide more fishing opportunity for anglers. We (WDFW) are working with the Yakama Nation to reintroduce sockeye (red) salmon. They have been extinct in the Yakima Basin for over one hundred years because of the construction of irrigation storage reservoirs without fish passage by the federal government in the 1910–33 period. We are also working to increase runs of summer Chinook and coho salmon, steelhead, bull trout, and Pacific lamprey.

What are the biggest threats to fishes in Washington state, and how are you addressing that problem?

1. The loss of high-quality habitat associated with increasing population and development. I spend considerable time working with our habitat program, other agencies/tribes, and the Yakima Basin Fish & Wildlife Recovery Board on prioritizing habitat acquisition and/or restoration projects for funding.

2. Climate change is also a long-term threat to species like salmon, steelhead, and bull trout that require clean, cold water. As mountain snowpack declines (replaced with rainfall instead of snow), water supplies for agriculture, people, and fish are threatened, particularly in the summer (hence the need/impetus for the Yakima River Basin Integrated Water Management Plan).

In your career, what has been your biggest challenge?
Overcoming opposition by the irrigated agriculture industry to working with the fish restoration coalition to rebuild/recover salmon, steelhead, and other fishes in the Yakima Basin. The US Bureau of Reclamation and the irrigation districts own and operate storage reservoirs, diversion dams, and other infrastructure that alter the natural hydrology (timing, quantity, and quality of river flows) for the purpose of diverting water for out-of-stream use. The fish community strives to maintain a more natural water management regime that keeps sufficient water instream for fish and overall ecosystem health. In the 1980s and '90s, there was active opposition and legal action because of these conflicting uses. In recent years, the legal battles have subsided and both sides are working together.

What part of your work do you enjoy the most and why?
Successfully completing a project or assignment and knowing that I have done my best to produce a high-quality outcome or final product . . . whatever that may be. I am always thinking—how do I best use my work time to "add value" to the work and the desired product? This is the hallmark of a strong work ethic, which is what you need to exhibit to have a successful career path in any field, including working with fish and wildlife.

What tips would you give kids who are interested in pursuing a career working with fish or marine mammals?
Focus on math, science, and communication skills (oral and written) in school. Do not limit science studies to biology. Also, learn about chemistry, geology (earth sciences), physics, etc. Both classroom and field studies, if possible. Problem-solving and working collaboratively with others on a team (team-building) are very important skills for students to develop.

Regarding written communication, I am appalled by some entry-level professional staff's inability to clearly and concisely articulate their ideas in writing (vocabulary, spelling, grammar, sentence structure, etc.) in both technical and non-tech documents. Few people proofread and edit their work before hitting the "send" button (my big pet peeve).

Volunteer to do water quality monitoring or other "citizen science" projects in your community through youth organizations like Boy Scouts or Girl Scouts, or volunteer directly with your local department of fish and wildlife office.

What is your favorite animal and why?
Impossible to name just one. I would have to say all "anadromous" (migratory) species, such as Atlantic salmon, the six species of Pacific salmon found in Washington (Chinook, coho, pink, chum, sockeye, and steelhead), and Pacific lamprey. These migratory fishes spawn and live as juveniles for a time in freshwater, and then they migrate to the ocean to grow and reach maturity in saltwater. They then return to freshwater, often returning to the same place where they were born, to reproduce. They travel hundreds or thousands of miles and overcome tremendous obstacles to complete their life cycle. They face many predators, such as birds, other fish, marine mammals, and man, and many obstacles, such as dams, waterfalls, low flows, and poor water quality, to achieve their goal. They are amazing creatures!

|||||||||||||||||||||||||||||||||||||||||||||||||||||||||||||||||||||||||||||||||||||||||||||||||||||||||||||

Aquatic or Marine Biologist

To be an aquatic or marine biologist, you will need at least a bachelor's degree, but plan to get a master's degree or even a doctorate. The early college track is similar for both specialties, with classes in biology, chemistry, physics, and math. It's when you start taking electives that things begin to change. Aquatic biologists will take classes like freshwater ecology, freshwater invertebrate zoology, or limnology, which is the study of inland waters. Marine biologists take classes like oceanography, marine botany, or deep sea biology. And being a certified scuba diver is useful if you want to do deep-water research.

Where Aquatic or Marine Biologists Work

With a bachelor's degree:

- 🐾 field assistant

- 🐾 fish hatchery technician

- 🐾 laboratory technician

- 🐾 primary or secondary school biology classes (need a teaching certificate)

- 🐾 non-academic researcher

With a master's degree or doctorate:

- 🐾 aquariums

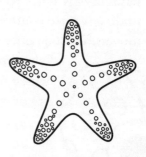

- 🐾 colleges or universities (as professors or research scientists)

- 🐾 environmental agencies

- 🐾 fisheries (aquaculturist is the name for fish farmers)

- 🐾 government agencies

- 🐾 international agencies like the United Nations (marine biologists)

- museums (taxonomists identify species of fish, including fish fossils)

- private companies

> The Frozen Zoo at the San Diego Zoo Safari Park is a collection of more than 8,400 DNA samples from more than eight hundred near-extinct species of animals. Sperm, eggs, embryos, and tissue cells are collected and stored in tanks of liquid nitrogen. This genetic material is later reprogrammed into stem cells for long-term preservation so that one day these stem cells may save animals from extinction through in vitro fertilization and cloning.

Insect Biologists

Entomologists study bugs. They do everything from finding and naming new bugs, to studying insect behaviors and life cycles, to finding ways to control those insects that are considered pests. Most universities don't offer a bachelor's degree in entomology, but some offer a minor in the subject. Plan to get your bachelor's degree in biology, zoology, or a related field. Then, if you are interested in research or teaching, go on to get a master's degree and probably a doctoral degree in entomology. The Entomological Society of America has two certifications. The Associate Certified Entomologist (ACE) is for those who have hands-on training in pest management, and the Board Certified Entomologist (BCE) is for those whose experience comes from academic study.

What do entomologists study?

- benefits of insects like ladybugs, wasps, and honeybees

- bug anatomy and bodily functions

- bug behavior

- bug migration and distribution around the world

- bug life cycles

- human and veterinary pests and how to control them

- newly discovered bugs and their classification

- urban, forest, and agricultural pests

Where Entomologists Work

- agricultural companies, farms, and other commercial companies to help protect crops, lawns, and buildings from invasive insects

- colleges and universities, teaching classes and conducting research

- Cooperative Extension Services (an agency of the Federal Department of Agriculture), educating farmers, urban businesses, homeowners, and others about insect management

- federal government, as regulatory entomologists—keeping foreign bugs out of the country, quarantining areas where invasive insects have settled to stop their spread, and enforcing laws and providing technical information to other insect control groups

- insecticide companies, developing new products

- law enforcement, as forensic entomologists who specialize in insect life cycles and behavior to determine time and cause of death at crime scenes

- medical and public health agencies, to help control pests like lice, ticks, and cockroaches

- military, to control pests on bases around the world

- timber industry, to protect trees from pests

- zoos and botanical gardens, to manage insect exhibits and control invasive insects

Other Wildlife Research Positions

Field assistants usually work for a few months, often in the summer. They do whatever jobs the researchers (master's and doctoral degree–seeking students) need them to do. They find nests, count animals, observe behaviors, and collect samples. Field assistants need a strong interest in animals, attention to detail, and a willingness to work long hours. This job is a great way to show your interest in a specific animal if you want to pursue a master's or doctoral degree.

Field research technicians have some scientific experience or a bachelor's degree in an animal-related field. They assist researchers in the field, collecting data and observing animals in their natural habitats.

Dame Jane Goodall (1934–), British Primatologist, Ethologist, Anthropologist, and United Nations Messenger of Peace.

Jane Goodall was born on April 3, 1934, the elder of two girls who were born on the same day but four years apart. Jane and her sister were raised in London, England, and attended Upland private school, where Jane earned her graduation certificate in 1952.

When Goodall was a toddler, her mother gave her a stuffed chimpanzee that she named Jubilee. That toy, which she has kept close her entire life, was the beginning of a deep fascination with primates. By the time she was eight she was obsessed, and after reading *Dr. Doolittle* by Hugh Lofting, she knew she had to go to Africa.

Even her early interest in animals focused on their behavior. At the age of four, she hid in the chicken coop so she could see how chickens laid their eggs. As she grew, she spent her free time watching birds and animals, sketching them and taking copious notes. Then, when she was twelve, she started her own society, the Alligator Club. Everything she did was training for her dream job, observing exotic animals in their native habitats.

Through a string of events and the help of friends, Goodall met anthropologist Louis Leakey, the curator of the Coryndon Museum in Nairobi, Africa. He hired her as his secretary and took her on an archeological dig to Olduvai Gorge, a site that is famous for its fossilized remains of early humans. Leaky gave her a chance to study the vervet monkey in the wild, and he encouraged her to consider studying chimpanzees.

Leakey told her that the best way to conduct a study was to live with the animals and observe them for a long period of time. Before long, Goodall agreed to live with the chimps, and Leakey began to look for funding for what would later be called the Gombe Reserve project. This project is still going on today, fifty years later, and monitors the daily life of over one hundred chimpanzees.

Goodall started the Gombe Reserve project in 1960 by setting up camp on the shore of Lake Tanganyika. In the beginning, the chimps stayed far away. But because Goodall used nonthreatening behaviors and sat near their feeding area in the early mornings, they slowly began to tolerate her presence. It took about two years for them to get to the point where they would come up and accept a banana. Goodall called her daily banana feedings the "banana club."

By imitating the chimps' behaviors, climbing into trees, and eating their food, Goodall began to document behaviors that other scientists knew nothing about. She observed their complex social system, strong family ties, patterns of communication, and their ceremonial behaviors. She was the first to document chimps using tools, a skill that was previously thought to be unique to humans. They used stones as weapons and blades of grass like spoons to scoop up termites.

While studying chimps in Africa, Goodall met and married Dutch wildlife photographer Baron Hugo van Lawick. Besides their honeymoon trip, Goodall rarely left the camp. In 1965, she earned her PhD from Cambridge University—she is one of only eight people who earned that degree without completing a bachelor's degree first. Her doctoral thesis covered her first five years researching the chimps and was titled, "Behavior of the Free-Ranging Chimpanzee."

Goodall became a celebrity in 1965 after the release of the film *Miss Goodall and the Wild Chimpanzees* and because of her articles for *National Geographic* magazine. She was also well-respected in the scientific community because of her scientific journal articles. But it was her entertaining books that bridged the gap between science and the public by engaging readers and introducing her work to a wide audience. She used her fame to challenge scientists to rethink how they defined the differences between humans and primates.

Besides her chimp research and writing, Goodall also worked as a visiting professor at Stanford University from 1970 to 1975 and as an honorary visiting professor at the University of Dar es Salaam in Tanzania, a position she still holds. Her marriage to van Lawick ended in 1974, and a year later she married Tanzanian national parks director Derek Bryceson. He died in 1980.

The Jane Goodall Institute was established in 1977 to help support the Gombe Reserve project and raise awareness of the plight of chimpanzees. Today, Goodall's focus is on educating governments, businesses, and individuals about the loss of chimp habitat and the unethical treatment of chimps used for scientific research. Goodall said, "The more we learn of the true nature of nonhuman animals, especially those with complex brains and corresponding complex social behaviour, the more ethical concerns are raised regarding their use in the service of man."[1]

Goodall has received numerous awards for her work. She was named a Messenger of Peace by the United Nations in 2002 and a Dame of the British Empire by Queen Elizabeth II of England in 2003. She still travels hundreds of days a year, lecturing about her life's work and campaigning for the causes closest to her heart:

conservation, saving endangered species, and fighting illegal hunting.

Animals Used in Research

The most common animals used in research are mice, rats, fishes, and birds. The next largest group is guinea pigs, rabbits, and hamsters. After that, fewer numbers of primates, pigs, farm animals, dogs, and cats are used. The 1966 *Animal Welfare Act* and its amendments is a federal law that regulates the treatment of these animals. It protects only warm-blooded animals and excludes mice, rats, and birds. Animal research practices are enforced by the Animal Care agency, part of the United States Department of Agriculture's Animal and Plant Health Inspection Service.

The humane use of animals in scientific research follows these three rules, called the three Rs:

1. **Replace** the use of animals with alternative techniques, or avoid the use of animals altogether.

2. **Reduce** the number of animals used to a minimum, to obtain information from fewer animals or more information from the same number of animals.

3. **Refine** the way experiments are carried out, to make sure animals suffer as little as possible. This includes providing better housing and revising procedures to minimize pain and suffering and/or improve animal welfare.

All scientists who wish to use animals for research must first explain why they need them, prove that there is no alternative, show how they will use as few animals as possible, and show how they will ease any suffering the animals might encounter. Animal protection organizations across the United States are working to stop all animal research. At this time, that isn't possible, but the three Rs are helping reduce the number used and encouraging researchers to think outside the box to find ways to do their research without using animals. In 2012, the National Institutes of Health announced that they would retire their 113 research chimpanzees to Chimp Haven, the National Chimpanzee Sanctuary in Louisiana.

About twenty miles east of Death Valley National Park, in the Ash Meadows National Wildlife Refuge, there live tiny iridescent blue fish that are beloved by many conservationsts and scientists. They are the Pupfish of Devils Hole. These fish are considered the rarest fish on earth with fewer than 200 of them swimming in the 93 degree waters of the cavern. At only one inch long, they are genetically the same as their ancestors that got trapped in the cavern between ten and twenty thousand years ago! In an effort to protect the species from extinction, Devils Hole became part of Death Valley National Park and the fish are on the endangered species list.

Quiz: Guess the Groups

Most people are familiar with the names for some groups of animals. For instance, a group of lions is a pride, a group of doves is a flock, and a group of wild dogs is a pack. But did you know that a group of cats is a clowder, a group of crows is a murder, and a group of flamingos is a flamboyance? Sometimes the names for groups of animals are delightfully unfamiliar! Using this true-or-false quiz, you can learn the names of some unfamiliar groups and then dazzle your friends with your knowledge.

1. A *congregation* is a group of alligators.

2. A *battery* is a group of barracudas.

3. A *bellowing* is a group of elephants.

4. A *knot* is a group of birds.

5. An *intrigue* is a group of wild cats.

6. A *quiver* is a group of cobras.

7. A *mischief* is a group of moles.

8. A *dazzle* is a group of giraffes.

9. A *gaze* is a group of raccoons.

10. A *skulk* is a group of skunks.

Answers

1. True—look for an alligator walking down the aisle the next time you go to your church, mosque, or temple.

2. True—next time you ask for new *batteries* for the remote control, you could get a group of aggressive tropical fish instead.

3. False—a group of elephants is called a *memory* or a *herd*. A bellowing refers to a group of bullfinches—small birds that can imitate human melodies. Teaching these birds was a popular pastime in the eighteenth and nineteenth centuries.

4. False—a *knot* is the name for a group of frogs, toads, or snakes. Groups of birds are called different names depending on their species: a *wreck* of sea birds, a *flock* of ground birds, an *exaltation* of larks, or a *murmuration* of starlings.

5. False—a group of wild cats is called a *destruction*. An *intrigue* is another name for a group of kittens, just like *litter* or *kindle*. And speaking of cats, a group of feral domestic cats is called a *colony* or a *clowder*, and a group of house cats can be called a *pounce* or—my favorite—a *nuisance*.

6. True—but that isn't the kind of *quiver* you want to carry your arrows in!

7. False—groups of moles are called *labors, companies,* or *movements*. However, it is rare to find moles in groups because they are very territorial. The word *mischief* is what you call a group of mice.

8. False—a group of giraffes is called a *tower*. A *dazzle* is the name for a group of zebras, along with a *cohort* or a *zeal*. Bring these words with you the next time you visit the zoo.

9. True—they're also, though less often, called a *nursery*.

10. False—a group of skunks is a *surfeit*. A *skulk* refers to a group of foxes.

Resources

About Animals

Animal Fact Guide, www.animalFactGuide.com
Association of Zoos and Aquariums, www.aza.org
Easy Science for Kids, http://easyscienceforkids.com/animals
International Wolf Center, www.wolf.org
Kids Biology, www.kidsbiology.com
National Geographic Kids, http://kids.nationalgeographic.com
One More Generation, http://onemoregeneration.org/
San Diego Zoo Kids, Kids.SanDiegoZoo.org
Wildscreen Arkive, www.arkive.org
World Wildlife Federation, www.worldwildlife.org

The Encyclopedia of Animals by David Alderton (Chartwell Books, 2013)
The Mysteries of Animal Intelligence: True Stories of Animals with Amazing Abilities by Sherry Hansen Steiger and Brad Steiger (Macmillan, 2007)
National Geographic Animal Encyclopedia: 2,500 Animals with Photos, Maps, and More! by Lucy H. Spelman (National Geographic Books, 2012)

About Animal Training

American Kennel Club, www.akc.org

How to Speak Cat: A Guide to Decoding Cat Language by
   Aline Alexander Newman and Gary Weitzman (National
   Geographic Books, 2015)
How to Speak Dog: A Guide to Decoding Dog Language by
   Aline Alexander Newman and Gary Weitzman (National
   Geographic Books, 2013)
How to Speak Dolphin by Ginny Rorby (Scholastic Press, 2015)
Kids Making a Difference for Animals by Nancy Furstinger and
   Sheryl L. Pipe (Wiley Publishing, Inc., 2009)
Puppy Training for Kids by Colleen Pelar (Barron's Educational
   Series, Inc., 2012)

About Bugs, Birds, and Fishes

The Adventures of Herman, http://extension.illinois.edu/worms/
Amateur Entomologists' Society, www.amentsoc.org/bug-club
American Birding Association Young Birders, http://
   youngbirders.aba.org
Bee Girl, www.beegirl.org
The Bug Chicks, www.thebugchicks.com
Fishing by *Boy's Life*, http://fishing.boyslife.org
Insects.org, www.insects.org
Audubon, www.audubon.org
Young Birders Network, http://ebird.org/content/ybn/

Insect Life by Arabella B. Buckley (Dodo Press, 2008)
*National Geographic Kids Bird Guide of North America: The Best
   Birding Book for Kids from National Geographic's Bird Experts!* by
   Jonathan Alderfer (National Geographic Books, 2013)

Ultimate Bugopedia: The Most Complete Bug Reference Ever by Darlyne Murawski and Nancy Honovich (National Geographic Books, 2013)

About Farmers

Agricultural Research Service, United States Department of Agriculture, www.ars.usda.gov/is/kids
FFA, www.ffa.org/home
4-H, www.4-h.org
National Young Farmers Coalition, www.youngfarmers.org

Barnyard Kids: A Family Guide for Raising Animals by Dina Rudick (Quarry Books, 2015)
Farming, Ranching, and Agriculture by Connor Syrewicz (Mason Crest, 2014)
How to Raise Goats: Everything You Need to Know by Carol Amundson (Voyageur Press, 2013)
A Kid's Guide to Keeping Chickens by Melissa Caughey (Storey Publishing, 2015)
Milk!: Life on a Dairy Farm by Ruth Owen (Windmill Books, 2012)
Pig Farmer by Jenna Lee Gleisner (The Child's World, 2015)

About Rodeos

American Junior Rodeo Association, www.ajra.org
National High School Rodeo Association, www.nhsra.com
National Little Britches Rodeo Association, www.nlbra.com

Calf Roping by Kimberly King (The Rosen Publishing Group, Inc., 2006)
The Cowgirl Way: Hats Off to America's Women of the West by Holly George-Warren (Houghton Mifflin Books for Children, 2010)

About Veterinarians

Vet Set Go, www.vetsetgo.com

Wildlife Vets International, www.wildlifevetsinternational.org

Career as a Veterinarian: What They Do, How to Become One, and What the Future Holds! by Brian Rogers (KidLit-O Books, 2013)

ER Vets: Life in an Animal Emergency Room by Donna M. Jackson (Sandpiper, 2009)

Vet Volunteers series by Laurie Halse Anderson

About Working Dogs

Animals at Work by Liz Palika and Katherine A. Miller (Wiley Publishing, Inc., 2009)

Dogs on Duty: Soldiers' Best Friends on the Battlefield and Beyond by Dorothy Hinshaw Patent (Bloomsbury USA, 2014)

Military Animals with Dog Tags by Laurie Calkhoven (Scholastic Inc., 2015)

Paws of Courage: True Tales of Heroic Dogs That Protect and Serve by Nancy Furstinger (National Geographic Children's Books, 2016)

Police Dogs by Mary Ann Hoffman (Gareth Stevens Publishing, 2011)

Animal Stories

Battle Bugs series by Jack Patton

Cracker!: The Best Dog in Vietnam by Cynthia Kadohata (Athenium Books for Young Readers, 2008)

Devoted: 38 Extraordinary Tales of Love, Loyalty, and Life with Dogs by Rebecca Ascher-Walsh (National Geographic Books, 2013)

A Dog's Life: The Autobiography of a Stray by Ann M. Martin (Scholastic Inc., 2005)

An Elephant in the Garden by Michael Morpurgo (Square Fish, 2013)

Heart of a Dolphin by Catherine Hapka (Scholastic Inc., 2016)

Maybe a Fox by Kathi Appelt and Alison McGhee (Athenum Books for Young Readers, 2016)

Mrs. Frisby and the Rats of NIMH by Robert C. O'Brien (Aladdin Paperbacks, 1986)

Nubs: The True Story of a Mutt, a Marine & a Miracle by Brian Dennis, Kirby Larson, and Mary Nethery (Little, Brown Books for Young Readers, 2009)

Old Wolf by Avi (Athenum Books for Young Readers, 2015)

The One and Only Ivan by Katherine Applegate (HarperCollins, 2015)

One Came Home by Amy Timberlake (Yearling, 2014)

Pax by Sara Pennypacker (Balzer + Bray, 2016)

Rain Reign by Ann M. Martin (Feiwel and Friends, 2014)

Rodeo Girl series by Suzanne D. Williams

The Saddle Club series by Bonnie Bryant

Stubby the War Dog: The True Story of World War I's Bravest Dog by Ann Bausum (National Geographic Books, 2014)

The Thing about Jellyfish by Ali Benjamin (Little, Brown and Company, 2015)

Turn Left at the Cow by Lisa Bullard (Houghton Mifflin Harcourt, 2015)

Unusual Chickens for the Exceptional Poultry Farmer by Kelly Jones (Random House Children's Books, 2015)

War Horse by Michael Morpurgo (Scholastic Inc., 2010)

The War That Saved My Life by Kimberly Brubaker Bradley (Dial Books for Young Readers, 2015)

Wringer by Jerry Spinelli (Harper Trophy, 1998)

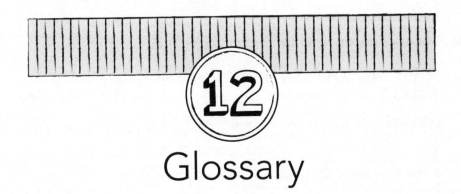

Glossary

abolitionist: a person who wants to end a practice or institution like slavery or the death penalty

abroad: in a foreign country

accredited: to be officially recognized

ACT: American College Test, a standardized test to determine if a high school graduate is prepared for college-level work

analysis: the process of understanding something by dividing it into smaller parts

anatomy: the study of the parts of a living organism

anesthesia: the elimination of pain or other sensations through the use of drugs or other methods like nerve blocks

angler: a person who fishes with a rod and line, a fisherman

apprenticeship: on-the-job training with an established professional to learn a trade or profession

artificial insemination: an attempt to get a female animal pregnant without the assistance of a male animal

associate's degree: a two-year degree usually earned at a community college

bachelor's degree: a four-year degree earned at a college or university

biology: the study of life and living organisms

castration: a surgical or chemical process used to stop male animals from reproducing

coexist: to live together peacefully even though you disagree on certain matters

commissary: a place where food is prepared

conditioning: a learning process where a specific action is used to get a specific response

conformation: the shape or structure of an animal

conservation: the act of preserving, guarding, or protecting something

cryptorchid: a condition where one or both testicles have not moved into the bag of skin below the penis

CT scan: a computer-generated image that combines a series of X-ray images taken from different angles and creates cross-sectional images, or slices

curator: the keeper or custodian of a museum or other collection

data: facts collected and used for analysis

decibel: a unit used to measure the intensity of a sound

deduction: the process of learning something by considering a general set of facts and thinking about how something specific relates to them

discipline: a particular area of study, especially a subject studied at a college or university

disposition: the way an animal usually behaves—friendly, skittish, and so on

doctorate: the highest degree awarded by a college or university for advanced study in a specific field

domestic animal: an animal that is not wild and is kept as a pet or to produce food

ecosystem: all the living things in an area and the way they affect each other and the environment

empathetic: having the ability to imagine how someone else feels

endangered: animals or plants that may soon not exist because there are very few now alive

equerry: an officer in charge of the care of horses

euthanize: to kill an animal because it is very old or sick or because there is no one to take care of it

exotic animal: an animal kept as a pet that is generally thought of as a wild species

FFA: Future Farmers of America, a student organization for those interested in agriculture and leadership

4-H: a youth development and mentoring organization

genealogy: the study of an animal's family tree, going back as far as possible

genetics: the study of how characteristics of living things are passed through the genes from parent to child

genome: a complete set of genetic instructions found in living organisms

GPA: grade point average

grant: a sum of money given by the government, a university, or a private organization to another organization or person for a special purpose

humane: kind, caring, and sympathetic toward others, especially those who are suffering

ichthyologist: a person who studies fishes

internship: on-the-job training under the supervision of someone more experienced

irrigation: the act of supplying land with water so that crops or plants will grow

keratin: the hard, fiberous protein found in fur, feathers, hoofs, claws, and horns

licensure: the granting or regulation of licenses, especially for professionals

master's degree: a two- or three-year advanced-study degree earned after a bachelor's degree

menagerie: a collection of different animals that are kept, usually for people to see

migration: the movement of animals from one region to another and back again, according to the season of the year

molt: to shed old skin, feathers, hair, or shells to make room for a growing body

narcotic: a type of drug that causes sleep, used medically to lessen pain, and in some forms is used illegally

negotiate: to have a discussion with someone in order to reach an agreement

nutritional: containing a food substance your body can use

pathology: the scientific study of disease

pharmaceutical: connected with the science, preparation, and production of medicines

physiologist: a person who studies the way living things work

plover: a bird with a short tail and long legs that is found mainly by the sea

pollinate: to carry pollen from a male part of a flower to the female part of another flower of the same type

post traumatic stress disorder: a mental health condition that is triggered by experiencing or witnessing a terrifying event

practice: to do work of a particular type for which a lot of training is necessary

productivity: the rate at which an animal produces a product like honey or milk

realistic: possessing an understanding of how things truly are

reasoning: the process of thinking about something in order to make a decision

rehabilitation: the act of returning an animal to a healthy or usual condition or way of living

reproductive: relating to the production of new life

residency: a period of work, usually in a hospital, for a doctor to get practical experience and training in a special area of medicine

retina: the area at the back of the eye that receives light and sends an image to the brain so that one can see

sanctuary: a place where birds or animals can live under protection

SAT: a standardized test to determine if a high school graduate is prepared for college-level work, includes a section on mathematical skills and one on verbal skills (the letters no longer stand for anything; they formerly stood for Scholastic Assessment Test)

selective: careful in choosing

socialization: to train an animal to behave in a certain way that others think is suitable; to get an animal accustomed to a variety of environments

specialty: a subject that someone knows a lot about

technician: a worker trained with special skills or knowledge, especially in how to operate machines or equipment used in science

technologist: someone who works with a particular technology

thermoreceptors: specialized nerve cells that are able to detect differences in temperature

venomous: adjective used to describe some snakes, insects, and spiders that release a poisonous liquid when they bite

wean: the process of moving a baby animal from drinking only mother's milk to eating solid food

zoonosis (plural zoonoses): diseases that can pass from animals to humans

zoology: the scientific study of animals

ACKNOWLEDGMENTS

This is my fourth book in the Be What You Want series, and it's about time I said "THANK YOU!" to Lindsay Easterbrooks-Brown and Emmalisa Sparrow Wood for their support during the writing and editing process. You are amazing! And my thanks to Andrea, my faithful and hard-working research assistant. You always make our long days of research more fun.

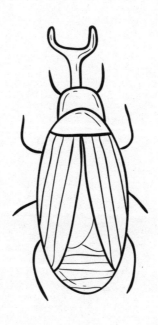

NOTES

Chapter 1

1. Malinda Larkin, "Pioneering a Profession: The Birth of Veterinary Education in the Age of Enlightenment," *Journal of the American Veterinary Medical Association*, December 19, 2010, under "Beginnings of a Revolution," https://www.avma.org/News /JAVMANews/Pages/110101a.aspx.

Chapter 2

1. "Dr. Louis J. Camuti, Cat Specialist," *New York Times*, February 27, 1981, http://www.nytimes.com/1981/02/27/obituaries/dr-louis -j-camuti-cat-specialist.html.

2. Donald F. Smith, "A Biography of and Interview about Louis J. Camuti, DVM: Class of 1920, New York University New York State Veterinary College," Cornell University An Enduring Veterinary Legacy collection, PDF, December 10, 2009: 3, https://ecommons.cornell.edu/bitstream/handle/1813/14197 /Camuti%2c%20Louis%20J.%20%2720%20BioInt.pdf?sequence =2&isAllowed=y.

Chapter 4

1. National Oceanic and Atmospheric Administration, "25 Years Later: Timeline of Recovery from the *Exxon Valdez* Oil Spill," NOAA Office of Response and Restoration, accessed April 12, 2016, http://response.restoration.noaa.gov/oil-and-chemical-spills /significant-incidents/exxon-valdez-oil-spill/timeline-ecological -recovery-infographic.html; "Questions and Answers about the Spill," Exxon Valdez Oil Spill Trustee Council, accessed April 12, 2016, http://www.evostc.state.ak.us/?FA=facts.QA.

Chapter 5

1. Alyssa Barnes, "5 Truths about Becoming a Cowboy," *Earn Your Spurs* (blog), February 7, 2015, http://www.earnyourspurs.com /how-to-be-a-cowboy/.
2. "Awards," National Cowgirl Museum and Hall of Fame, accessed February 23, 2016, http://www.cowgirl.net/hall-of-fame/awards/.
3. David L. Wykes, "Robert Bakewell, (1725–1795) of Dishley: Farmer and Livestock Improver," *The Agricultural History Review* 52, no. 1 (2004): 38-55.

Chapter 7

1. William Sauder, "How Two Women Ended the Deadly Feather Trade," *Smithsonian.com*, March 2013, http://www.smithsonianmag .com/science-nature/how-two-women-ended-the-deadly-feather -trade-23187277/?page=1&no-ist.
2. State of Missouri v. Holland, 252 U.S. 416, (April 19, 1920), Cornell University Law School website, https://www.law.cornell.edu /supremecourt/text/252/416#writing-USSC_CR_0252_0416_ZO.
3. Heather Gurd, "Inspiring Warriors to Conserve Lions in Kenya," *Cat Watch* (blog), *National Geographic*, June 19, 2015, http://voices .nationalgeographic.com/2015/06/19/inspiring-warriors-to -conserve-lions-in-kenya/.

4. Jerry Adler, "Kill All the Mosquitoes?!" *Smithsonian Magazine,* June 2016, http://www.smithsonianmag.com/innovation/kill-all -mosquitos-180959069/.

Chapter 8
1. Martha Teichner, "The Photo Ark: Preserving Species Before They Disappear," *CBS News,* November 15, 2015, http://www .cbsnews.com/news/the-photo-ark-preserving-species-before-they -disappear/.

Chapter 9
1. "Locust," *National Geographic,* accessed June 28, 2016, http:// animals.nationalgeographic.com/animals/bugs/locust/.
2. U.S. Department of Justice, "Service Animals," ADA 2010 Revised Requirements, July 12, 2011, https://www.ada.gov/service _animals_2010.htm.

Chapter 10
1. Jane Goodall, *Through a Window: 30 Years Observing the Gombe Chimpanzees* (New York: Houghton Mifflin, 1990), quoted in Carol Hand, *Jane Goodall* (New York: The Rosen Publishing Group, 2014), 89.

BIBLIOGRAPHY

Websites

American Society of Animal Science: https://asas.org/

American Veterinary Medical Association: www.avma.org

Anti-Persoonsmijnen Ontmijnende Product Ontwikkeling: www.apopo.org

Bureau of Labor Statistics, United States Department of Labor: www.bls.gov

Cambridge Dictionaries Online: http://dictionary.cambridge.org/us

Days of the Year: www.daysoftheyear.com

Dogs for Law Enforcement: www.dogsforlawenforcement.org

Guard from Above: http://guardfromabove.com

Jane Goodall Institute Research Center, "Gombe Chimpanzees": http://gombechimpanzees.org

Joel Sartore Photography Inc.: www.joelsartore.com

National Aviary of Pittsburgh: www.aviary.org/about-us

National Oceanic and Atmospheric Administration. www.nefsc.noaa.gov

Study.com: www.study.com

Temple Grandin, PhD: www.templegrandin.com

U.S. Fish and Wildlife Service: www.fws.gov

Articles and Books

Ashby, Ben. "Top 25 College Fishing Teams." Bassmaster. June 17, 2013. https://www.bassmaster.com/news/current -college-team-rankings.

Audubon. "History of the Christmas Bird Count." Accessed March 8, 2016. www.audubon.org/conservation/history-christmas -bird-count.

Audubon. "John James Audubon: The American Woodsman; Our Namesake and Inspiration." Accessed April 26, 2016. http:// www.audubon.org/content/john-james-audubon.

Avery, Breckyn. "Animal Rescue 101: Adopting from an Animal Rescue Vs. Shelter." Examiner.com. April 4, 2013. www .examiner.com/article/animal-rescue-101-adopting-from -an-animal-rescue-vs-shelter.

"Aviary Zookeeper." Warnell School of Forestry and Natural Resources, University of Georgia. Last updated March 19, 2012. https://jobs.forestry.uga.edu/aviary-zookeeper.

"Becoming a Zoo Veterinarian: Step-by-Step Career Guide." Study.com. Accessed February 12, 2016. http://study.com /articles/Becoming_a_Zoo_Veterinarian_Step-by-Step _Career_Guide.html.

"Beginning Falconry." The Avian Reconditioning Center. Accessed April 5, 2016. https://www.arc4raptors.org /beginning-falconry.html.

Bestoloffe, John. "A Day in the Life of a Texas Cowboy." Shale Plays Media. Accessed February 19, 2016. http://eaglefordtexas .com/day-life-texas-cowboy/.

Bienaimé, Pierre. "The US Navy's Combat Dolphins Are Serious Military Assets." Business Insider. March 12, 2015. http://www .businessinsider.com/the-us-navys-combat-dolphins-are -serious-military-assets-2015-3.

Biography.com editors. "Aristotle Biography." A&E Television Networks. Accessed January 8, 2016. www.biography.com /people/aristotle-9188415.

Biography.com editors. "Jane Goodall Biography." A&E
  Television Networks. Accessed April 1, 2016. http://www
  .biography.com/people/jane-goodall-9542363.

BirdNote. "Fake Marbled Murrelet Eggs Cause Jays to Vomit."
  Audubon. August 29, 2013. http://www.audubon.org/news
  /fake-marbled-murrelet-eggs-cause-jays-vomit.

Bishop, Gerry. "What Good Are Bugs?" *Ranger Rick.* Accessed
  May 3, 2016. https://www.nwf.org/Kids/Ranger-Rick
  /Animals/Insects-and-Arthropods/What-Good-Are-Bugs.aspx.

Blatty, David. "David Attenborough Biography." The Biography
  .com. A&E Television Networks, July 6, 2016. Accessed
  December 6, 2016. http://www.biography.com/people/
  david-attenborough.

Born, Fred J. "The Early History of the Horse Doctor: A Story
  Covering Over 2200 Years of the Evolution of the Study of
  Veterinary Medicine." PowerPoint created for Vet2011. 2011.
  Accessed January 8, 2016. www.avmhs.org/horse/early.history
  .horse.doctor11.pptx.

Buchheim, Jason. "A Quick Course in Ichthyology." Odyssey
  Expeditions. Accessed March 25, 2016. www.marinebiology
  .org/fish.

"A Connecticut Hero." Governor's Foot Guard. Accessed April
  19, 2016. http://www.governorsfootguard.com/stubby/.

Curth, Louise Hill. *'A Plaine and Easie Waie to Remedie a Horse':
  Equine Medicine in Early Modern England.* Leiden, The Netherlands: Koninklijke Brill NV, 2013. https://books.google.com
  /books?id=oRCaAAAAQBAJ&printsec=frontcover#v
  =onepage&q&f=false.

Daniels, Chris. "How do I become an Animal Control Officer?"
  Criminal Justice Degree Hub. Accessed February 1, 2016.
  www.criminaljusticedegreehub.com/how-do-i-become-an
  -animal-control-officer/.

"David Attenborough Biography." Internet Movie Database.
  Accessed December 6, 2016. http://www.imdb.com/name
  /nm0041003/.

De Trey-White, Simon. "The Unique Mawari Indian Indigenous Horse." http://simondetreywhite.photoshelter.com/image /I0000I.SoUV_Jwpg.

"Devils Hole." National Parks Service. Accessed August 8, 2016. https://www.nps.gov/deva/learn/nature/devils-hole.htm.

"Devils Hole Pupfish." U.S. Fish and Wildlife Service, Nevada Fish & Wildlife Office. Accessed August 8, 2016. https://www .fws.gov/nevada/protected_species/fish/species/dhp/dhp.html.

Dog Star Daily. "Dr. Ian Dunbar." Accessed February 5, 2016. www.dogstardaily.com/blogger/4.

Dogtime. "The Dog Trainer's Trainer." Dogtime.com. Accessed February 5, 2016. http://dogtime.com/dog-health/dog -behavior/1273-cesar-millan-and-ian-dunbar.

"Dr. Ian Dunbar." Forever Friends Dog Training. Accessed February 5, 2016. www.foreverfriendsdogtraining.com /dr-ian-dunbar.

Dunk, Marcus. "Bullets, Bread and Beer, Tambourines and Toothpaste . . . and the 180 Other Things You Can to Do with a Pig." *Daily Mail.* Last modified October 3, 2009. www .dailymail.co.uk/sciencetech/article-1217794/From-bullets -bread-beer-tambourines-toothpaste--plus-180-things-pig.html.

Eden, Bob. "So You Want to Be a K9 Handler?" Police One .com. September 2, 2000. https://www.policeone.com/K-9 /articles/44434-So-You-Want-to-Be-a-K9-Handler/.

Encyclopaedia Britannica Online. "Robert Bakewell: British Agriculturalist." Accessed February 25, 2016. www.britannica .com/biography/Robert-Bakewell.

"Entomologist." North Carolina Association for Biomedical Research. Accessed March 1, 2016. www.aboutbioscience.org /careers/entomologist.

FAO Fisheries and Aquaculture Department. "Strategy for Fisheries, Aquaculture and Climate Change." Food and Agriculture Organization of the United Nations. 2012. www .fao.org/3/a-at500e.pdf.

"Farmers, Ranchers, and Other Agricultural Managers." College Grad. Accessed February 19, 2016. https://collegegrad.com /careers/farmers-ranchers-and-other-agricultural-managers.

Freeman, Albert E. "Breeding." *Encyclopaedia Britannica Online.* Accessed June 13, 2016. www.britannica.com/science /animal-breeding.

Frobish, Nestle J. "Exotic Animals Deployed as Delta 'Weed Whackers.'" UC Davis Center for Watershed Sciences. April 1, 2015. https://californiawaterblog.com/2015/04/01 /exotic-herbivores-deployed-to-mow-down-waterweeds -clogging-delta/.

Ghose, Tia. "Why Earth's Largest Ape Went Extinct." *LiveScience.* January 11, 2016. http://www.livescience .com/53313-biggest-ape-forest-dweller.html.

Gray, Richard. "Eggstraordinary! Foot-Long Elephant Bird Egg Complete with Embryo Remains Could Fetch £50,000 at Auction." *Daily Mail.* March 19, 2015. http://www.dailymail .co.uk/sciencetech/article-3002369/Eggstraordinary-FOOT -LONG-elephant-bird-egg-complete-embryo-remains-fetch -50-000-auction.html.

Greenwood, Beth. "Wardens Vs. Rangers." The Nest. Accessed March 29, 2016. http://woman.thenest.com/wardens-vs -rangers-21674.html.

Hanna, Jack. *Jungle Jack: My Wild Life.* Nashville: Thomas Nelson, 2008.

Harness, Jill. "4 Animals You Can Only Find in Zoos." *Mental_Floss.* May 31, 2011. http://mentalfloss.com /article/27867/4-animals-you-can-only-find-zoos.

Heimbuch, Jaymi. "5 Owl Facts That Will Amaze You." Mother Nature Network. February 18, 2014. www.mnn.com /earth-matters/animals/stories/5-owl-facts-that-will-amaze-you.

"A History of Falconry." International Association for Falconry and Conservation of Birds of Prey. Accessed April 5, 2016. http://www.iaf.org/HistoryFalconry.php.

"History of Origami." Origami Resource Center. Accessed April 11, 2016. http://www.origami-resource-center.com/history-of-origami.html.

"History of the APDT." The Association of Professional Dog Trainers. Accessed February 5, 2016. https://apdt.com/about/history/.

"History of Zoos." Canadian Broadcasting Corporation. Accessed February 12, 2016. www.cbc.ca/doczone/features/history-of-zoos.

"How to Become a Beekeeper: Career Path Guide." Scholar Invest Inc. Accessed March 1, 2016. www.academicinvest.com/science-careers/biology-careers/how-to-become-a-beekeeper.

"How to Become a Wildlife Rehabilitator." PAWS. Accessed March 29, 2016. www.paws.org/library/wildlife/become-a-rehabilitator/.

"How to Start Out as a Wildlife Photographer." Discover Wildlife. Accessed April 7, 2016. http://www.discoverwildlife.com/how-start-out-wildlife-photographer.

Jarvis, Brooke. "Can Rocks and Paintballs Help Humans and Mountain Goats Coexist? An Alternative Approach to Wildlife Management in the Olympic National Forest." *High Country News.* November 13. 2013. https://www.hcn.org/issues/45.19/can-rocks-and-paintballs-help-humans-and-mountain-goats-coexist.

Jones, Abigail. "Jane Goodall's Jungles." *Newsweek.* October 23, 2014. http://www.newsweek.com/2014/10/31/jane-goodalls-jungles-279259.html.

Joyner, Jeffrey. "The Disadvantages of Being a Game Warden." *Houston Chronicle.* Accessed March 29, 2016. http://work.chron.com/disadvantages-being-game-warden-26383.html.

"K-9's That Died While Still in Service." Connecticut Police Department Work Dog Association. Accessed April 18, 2016. http://www.cpwda.com/k9_kilod.htm.

Kruzer, Adrienne. "Top 10 Bad Pets: 10 Animals to Avoid Keeping as a Pet." About.com. Last modified September 4,

2015. http://exoticpets.about.com/od/choosinganexoticpet/tp
/TopTenAnimalsThatShouldNotBeKeptAsPets.htm.

"The Lahun Papyri." University College London. Accessed January 8, 2016. www.ucl.ac.uk/museums-static/digitalegypt//
lahun/papyri.html.

Larkin, Malinda. "Pioneering a Profession: The Birth of
Veterinary Education in the Age of Enlightenment." *Journal of
the American Veterinary Medical Association.* December 19, 2010.
https://www.avma.org/News/JAVMANews/Pages/110101a
.aspx.

Lang, Leslie. "5 Amazing Facts You Never Knew about the
American Cowboy." Ancestery. Accessed June 13, 2016.
http://blogs.ancestry.com/cm/2015/02/20/5-amazing-facts
-you-never-knew-about-the-american-cowboy/.

Lights, Zion. "10 Global Sanctuaries That Are Transforming the
Lives of Animals." Onegreenplanet.org. April 8, 2013. www
.onegreenplanet.org/animalsandnature/10-global-sanctuaries
-that-are-transforming-the-lives-of-animals/.

Lovato, Frank Jr. "What It Takes to Be a Jockey." Horsejobs
.ca. July 16, 2009. www.horsejobs.ca/blog/?p=5. Previously
published in *Horses,* August 2008.

McLendon, Russell. "7 Examples of Animal Democracy."
Mother Nature Network. November 4, 2012. http://www
.mnn.com/earth-matters/animals/photos/7-examples-of
-animal-democracy/democracy-takes-flight.

Miller, Kathie. "Falconry: The Art of Hunting Using Birds of
Prey as Your Partner." *The Art of Falconry.* Accessed April 5,
2016. https://falconryart.wordpress.com/.

Mitchell, John H. "The Mothers of Conservation." Special issue,
Sanctuary: *The Journal of the Massachusetts Audubon Society.*
January/February 1996. www.massaudubon.org/content
/download/11638/186451/file/FoundingMothers-mass
-audubon.pdf.

"Mr Bourgelat Claude." World Veterinary Heritage. Last
modified May 21, 2015. http://world-veterinary-heritage.org

/base/bourgelat.php?menu=voir_h&id2=793&lang=en&
affichage=grand.

NCC Staff. "Honoring the First Dog to Be Awarded the Purple
Heart." Constitution Daily. March 13, 2015. http://blog
.constitutioncenter.org/2015/03/honoring-the-only-dog-to
-be-awarded-the-purple-heart/.

"Ophthalmology." VCA Northwest Veterinary Specialists.
Accessed January 19, 2016. www.vcaspecialtyvets.com
/northwest-veterinary-specialists/departments-doctors
/departments/ophthalmology.

Paull, Jennifer. "Trend Watch: Retirement Homes for Pets."
Vetstreet. July 9, 2012. www.vetstreet.com/our-pet-experts
/trend-watch-retirement-homes-for-pets.

Plank, Alex. "Interview with Temple Grandin." Wrong Planet.
January 2, 2006. http://wrongplanet.net/interview-with
-temple-grandin.

Quammen, David. "Being Jane Goodall." *National Geographic.*
October 2012. http://ngm.nationalgeographic.com/2010/10
/jane-goodall/quammen-text.

"Robert Bakewell (1725–1795)." BBC. Accessed February 25,
2016. www.bbc.co.uk/history/historic_figures/bakewell
_robert.shtml.

"Salary and Career Options for Veterinary Assistants." Veterinary
Medicine Careers. Accessed January 30, 2016. http://veterinary
medicinecareers.org/salary-and-career-options-for-veterinary
-assistants/.

Salter, Susan. "Krone, Julie." In *Notable Sports Figures.* Reprint
of the 2004 Gale Group edition, Encyclopedia.com. Accessed
April 8, 2016. http://www.encyclopedia.com/topic/Julie
_Krone.aspx.

Savoca, Matthew. "Seabirds' Plastic-Eating Habits Remain
Puzzling." Live Science Expert Voices. November 10, 2016.
http://www.livescience.com/56815-why-do-seabirds-eat-
plastic.html.

Schreiber, Barbara A. "Jack Hanna: American Zoologist and
Television Personality." *Encyclopaedia Britannica Online.* Last

modified September 1, 2014. www.britannica.com/biography
/Jack-Hanna.

Sebastian, Nick. "10 Fascinating Pets of Powerful World Leaders." ListVerse. April 10, 2014. http://listverse.com/2014/04
/10/10-fascinating-pets-of-powerful-world-leaders/.

Simon, Matt. "Absurd Creature of the Week: The Feisty Shrimp
That Kills with Bullets Made of Bubbles." *WIRED*. July 11,
2014. www.wired.com/2014/07/absurd-creature-of-the-week
-pistol-shrimp/.

Simon, Matt. "Absurd Creature of the Week: The Incredible
Critter That's Tough Enough to Survive in Space." *WIRED*.
March 21, 2014. http://www.wired.com/2014/03/absurd
-creature-week-water-bear/.

Smith, Donald F. "Louis J. Camuti, the First Feline Veterinarian:
He Dignified the Cat." *Veritas*. May 28, 2013. www
.veritasdvmblog.com/louis-j-camuti-the-first-feline
-veterinarian-he-dignified-the-cat/.

Smith, Wesley D. "Hippocrates: Greek Physician." *Encyclopaedia
Britannica Online*. Accessed January 8, 2016. www.britannica
.com/biography/Hippocrates.

Strauss, Mark. "The Largest Ape That Ever Lived Was Doomed
By Its Size." *National Geographic*. January 5, 2016. http://news
.nationalgeographic.com/2016/01/160106-science-evolution
-apes-giant/.

"Stubby the Military Dog." State of Connecticut. Last modified
March 13, 2015. http://www.ct.gov/mil/cwp/view.asp?a=1351
&q=257892.

Tan, Avianne. "Long-Lost Footage of 'Parachuting Beavers'
Found in Idaho." *ABC News*. October 23. 2015. http://abc
news.go.com/US/long-lost-historic-footage-parachuting
-beavers-dropped-airplanes/story?id=34682675.

Teichner, Martha. "The Photo Ark: Preserving Species before
They Disappear." *CBS News*. November 15, 2015. http://www
.cbsnews.com/news/the-photo-ark-preserving-species-before
-they-disappear/.

The Telegraph. "Ferrets Key to Bridging the Digital Divide between Cities and Rural Areas." April 1, 2010. http://www .telegraph.co.uk/news/newstopics/howaboutthat/7541455 /Ferrets-key-to-bridging-the-digital-divide-between-cities -and-rural-areas.html.

"10 Largest, Biggest & Best Aquariums In the World." Conservation Institute. Accessed February 12, 2016. www .conservationinstitute.org/10-largest-biggest-best-aquariums -in-the-world/.

"The Three Rs." Understanding Animal Research. Last modified November 18, 2014. http://www.understanding animalresearch.org.uk/how/three-rs/.

"The Truth About Sanctuaries." Global Federation of Animal Sanctuaries. Accessed March 22, 2016. www.sanctuary federation.org/gfas/for-public/truth-about-sanctuaries/.

"Types of War Dogs." The United States War Dog Association, Inc. Accessed April 18, 2016. http://www.uswardogs.org /war-dog-history/types-war-dogs/.

U.S. Customs and Border Protection. "Agriculture Canine." Department of Homeland Security. Accessed April 19, 2016. http://www.cbp.gov/border-security/protecting-agriculture /agriculture-canine.

"Veterinarians—What They Do." Studentscholarships.org. Accessed January 15, 2016. www.studentscholarships.org /salary/478/veterinarians.php.

"Veterinary Science." In *Encyclopaedia Britannica: A Dictionary of Arts, Sciences, Literature and General Information*. 11th ed. 29 vols. New York: The Encyclopedia Britannica Company, 1911. https://books.google.com/books?id=vf8tAAAAIAAJ&pg=PA3 &lpg=PA3&dq=Apsyrtus+of+Bithynia.

Wade, Nicholas. "Study Traces Cat's Ancestry to Middle East." *The New York Times*. June 29, 2007. www.nytimes.com/2007 /06/29/science/29cat.html.

"What Is a Ranch Manager?" Environmental Science.org. Accessed February 19, 2016. www.environmentalscience .org/career/ranch-manager.

"What Is an Orinthologist?" EnvironmentalScience.org
. Accessed March 8, 2016. www.environmentalscience.org
/career/ornithologist.

Wolf, A.V., Phoebe G. Prentiss, Lillian G. Douglas, and Russell
J. Swett. "Potability of Sea Water with Special Reference to
the Cat." *American Journal of Physiology* 196 (February 28, 1959):
633–641. http://ajplegacy.physiology.org/content/196/3/633.

Yeoman, Barry. "What Do Birds Do for Us?" *Audubon*. April 8,
2013. https://www.audubon.org/news/what-do-birds-do-us.

Yong, Ed. "A Genetic Study Writes a New Origin Story for
Dogs." *The Atlantic*. October 19, 2015. www.theatlantic.com
/science/archive/2015/10/genetic-study-writes-yet-another
-origin-story-for-dogs/411196/.

Zelevansky, Nora. "10 Surprising Things About How Animals
Sleep." Vet Street. May 14, 2012. http://www.vetstreet.com
/our-pet-experts/10-surprising-things-about-how-animals
-sleep.

"Zoo Statistics." Statistic Brain. April 8, 2015. www
.statisticbrain.com/zoo-statistics/.

"Zoo: Zoological Park." In *National Geographic Encyclopedia*,
edited by Kara West and Jeanie Evers. *National Geographic*. Last
updated July 22, 2011. http://education.nationalgeographic.org
/encyclopedia/zoo/.